AN INTRODUCTION TO JUDO

AN
INTRODUCTION
TO JUDO

GARY MURRAY

FOREWORD BY KEITH REMFRY,
BLACK BELT 7th DAN AND OLYMPIC MEDALLIST

ILLUSTRATED BY BEN MURRAY

An OPTIMA book

© Gary Murray 1989

First published in 1989 by
Macdonald Optima, a division of
Macdonald & Co. (Publishers) Ltd

A member of Maxwell Pergamon Publishing Corporation plc

British Library Cataloguing in Publication Data
Murray, Gary
    An introduction to judo. – (Martial arts series)
    1. Judo – Manuals
    I. Title   II. Series
    796.8'152

    ISBN 0-356-17856-0

Macdonald & Co. (Publishers) Ltd
66-73 Shoe Lane
Holborn
London EC4P 4AB

Photoset in 11pt Century Schoolbook by Leaper & Gard Ltd, Bristol, England

Printed and bound in Great Britain
by The Guernsey Press Co. Ltd., Guernsey, Channel Islands.

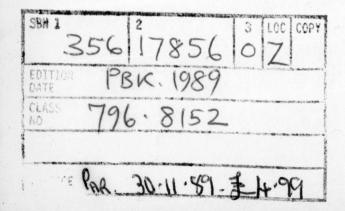

DEDICATION

This book is dedicated to the
late Dr Jigoro Kano, the
creator of judo — the gentle Way.

CONTENTS

PREFACE

In the 20th century, martial arts world-wide have combined to create a multi-million dollar industry. Annual subscriptions, the sale of equipment, as well as government financial aid has resulted in colossal amounts of money changing hands every year. Unfortunately, this trend has encouraged a severe degradation of the fundamental principles of certain martial arts, with a modern emphasis directed to winning sporting tournaments.

An Introduction to Judo examines the creation and expansion of one of the world's most popular Japanese martial arts. By explaining the traditional aims and philosophy of the founder, Dr Jigoro Kano, I hope readers will appreciate that the ultimate aim of the art of judo (the gentle Way) was never intended to be success in sporting tournaments, rather the development of the character of its participants.

FOREWORD

Why should anyone have to write a book introducing a
Japanese Olympic sport that can be practised by children
and adults? Surely a sport is a sport. Reading this book
will certainly change your mind about judo. To some
people it is an excuse to wrestle and throw opponents. To
others judo has taught them a code of ethics by which
they run their lives.

The Japanese often draw comparisons between Britain
and their country. In their opinion the countries and their
populations are similar. Both countries are islands off
large land masses and have experienced extreme feudal
regimes in their respective pasts. Is this why judo appeals
in ever increasing numbers to the British population? Or is
this the reason why judo is one of Britain's most
successful Olympic sports? Since 1972 the men's British
Judo Team has consistently brought home medals from
each Olympic Games. And competitive judo is not only for
men; British women's judo has led the world in recent
years and in doing so has produced a crop of World
Champions.

Increasingly, instructors are also asked about the use of
judo as a method of self defence. Like all combat/martial
arts it can be useful as part of an armoury of unarmed
skills which can be used in the defence of one's life. It is
not the ultimate unarmed self defence method — nothing
is. Anybody who says that their particular method is the
ultimate system should be ignored. It is much better to
have a good knowledge of several methods of defence
rather than to rely on one.

However, judo is not only about high-level competition
and self defence; it is functional at all levels. There are
physical and mental gains for everyone. Physically, judo
can be as strenuous as you wish to make it. The benefits
are both aerobic and anaerobic. It also helps develop good
balance and co-ordination.

Mentally, judo has many attributes. The timid gain confidence and bullies become respectful, realizing that their size does not count for everything. Others consider that judo is a game of chess played in the mind as you anticipate your opponent's movements and attempt to 'read their thoughts'. This is why blind people take part in the art so successfully and instructors have tried to imitate blind persons' abilities by encouraging full-sighted students to practise with their eyes shut.

The results are dramatic. In judo there is no chance to hide as there may be in a team sport. There is just you and your opponent locked in physical and mental combat in the middle of a twelve metre square contest area. Victory and defeat can be easily observed and the result is directly attributable to you.

The character qualities developed by judo are fully appreciated in Japan. There, individualism is rare and people with such qualities must be recognized and put to good use in Japan's highly structured population and workforce. Consequently, 'talent scouts' attend judo competitions and 'head hunt' champions to join their particular area of Japanese industry, government or commerce. Many captains of Japanese industry have had a very successful previous career in judo or another martial art. In Britain it is often thought that exclusive, expensive public schools develop the type of character qualities referred to above. Perhaps this is why judo has been increasingly adopted by such schools as an alternative to boxing.

In all sports there are those who say that modern methods are best and the traditional methods are outdated. The author aligns himself to the traditional methods of teaching to which I also subscribe. Gary Murray's presentation of why he supports the 'old' approach is both honest and factual.

To sum up this book, I consider it to be an essential read for people who are contemplating taking up judo or for parents who have enrolled their children for judo lessons at a local club. One thing is for sure, once you have sampled judo and realize the background to the art your life will never be the same.

I have competed at a very high level in judo but now, in my post-judo contest retirement period, I have found the lessons learnt help me with my family relationships, business dealings and attitude to and ability to cope with life. But, I also realize, that having travelled this far in my judo career I have a long way to go which will provide me with an interest for the rest of my life.

Keith Remfry,
Black Belt 7th Dan,
Olympic Silver Medallist.

1
HISTORY

The conception and evolution of the Japanese martial art judo must surely be one of the most extraordinary phenomena of the 20th century. And it is difficult to comprehend that a once lethal fighting system of *samurai* warriors has been transformed into a modern-day Olympic sport.

In order to understand the history of judo, it is necessary, first of all, to examine briefly the social and political environment of mid-19th-century Japan. At that time the commander-in-chief of the Japanese army was known notoriously throughout the nation as the *shogun.* This rank gave the holder effective control of Japan, even above the Emperor, who was the formal sovereign. The shogunate ran unbroken from 1192 to 1867, and was particularly noted for its unlimited military power.

However, the year 1867 was a period of revolutionary change for Japan, politically and socially. This situation was created by the defeat of the Tokugawa shogunate, followed by the restoration of imperial rule. The result was a winding-down of numerous feudal systems and arts, leaving the 'new' Japan hungry for 'modern', Western influences. As a part of this transformation was the gradual decline of *samurai* martial arts, in particular the combat schools of *ju-jitsu.* Many of these schools, despite being strongly entrenched at various clan capitals located throughout the country, found themselves tottering on the brink of ruin, there no longer being a need to practise the lethal art of unarmed combat.

SAMURAI WARRIORS

Indirectly, the *samurai* warriors of Japan contributed to the creation of judo. It is therefore important to understand a little of the background of this *corps élite*.

In simple terms a *samurai* can best be described as a highly-skilled academic combatant, the ultimate warrior, who despite his awesome ability in combat was just as much at home taking part in the delicate tea ceremony or appreciating the beauty of cherry blossom. The main task of this élite military class was to serve and protect local *daimios* (feudal barons or military leaders). This they did with dedicated loyalty, living by their own special code of honour and integrity accompanied by an unbelievable fighting spirit. The loyalty of the *samurai* was such that they considered any failure good enough reason to sacrifice their lives by ritual suicide. Their skill at arms, for example with swords or the bow, as well as the lethal unarmed combat system of *ju-jitsu*, was well known throughout Japan.

Despite a violent lifestyle, the chivalrous code of the *samurai* included many qualities that were a tremendous contribution to the social order. Personal discipline, intellectualism, as well as honour, dedication to duty and integrity were all impressive characteristics of Japan's fighting scholars. And this attitude to life has become a permanent, integral part of Japanese society. It was the lethal fighting art of *ju-jitsu*, accompanied by this academic, honourable attitude to life, that encouraged the creation of judo.

Samurai training

Training systems adopted by the various *samurai* clans were not unlike traditional martial arts *dojos* (places of practice). Regular sessions of sword practice would be held, accompanied by archery and spear training. *Ju-jitsu* sessions (see opposite) were also a regular feature in the *samurai* training programme. Relying principally on his swordmanship, the *samurai* also excelled in archery, horse riding, ropework, swimming and *ju-jitsu*. These skills were acquired initially at provincial training schools and refined through experience in actual combat.

The violent, uncertain lifestyle of the *samurai* was such that most experience was gained from 'on the job' training. It was not uncommon for these warriors to engage in life or death struggles lasting for days at a time, and the inexperienced either quickly progressed in combat skills, or fell to the sword.

Different clans adopted their own training systems, based on tricks and special methods of combat. There was no regular-known systemized training for the formal qualification of *samurai* except dedication over a period, as well as the eventual development of skill at arms and combat.

Budo

The feudal system in Japan introduced numerous traditional methods of fighting into the social structure of the entire country. Skilful use of farm implements and home-made weapons created different systems of combat. As they developed and became popular with *samurai* and military clans, the word *Budo* was used to describe the many fighting arts. The word *budo* is still used in Japan and is an overall description of the various arts and concepts. A person studying *budo* is referred to as a *budoka*.

Bushido is frequently confused with *budo* and is mistaken for an actual system of combat. This is not so: *bushido* is a moral, ethical code of conduct created in the 14th century by the *Bushi* (Knights of feudal Japan).

Ju-jitsu

This method of unarmed combat was developed and systematized by *samurai* masters skilled in different ways of fighting. For many years, *ju-jitsu* was accepted as the official system of self defence, and even today in Japan small groups still practise traditional aspects of this art. The substance of *ju-jitsu* includes throwing, immobilizing an opponent on the ground, kicking, as well as punching to vital parts of the body, choking, and locking the limbs of an adversary.

At one stage, there were over a hundred *ju-jitsu* schools operating in various areas of Japan. *Samurai* masters famous for their particular style cultivated thousands of followers. Some of these students became so skilful they eventually opened their own training establishments, becoming masters in their own right.

THE CONCEPTION OF JUDO

During the year 1871 two incidents occurred that were subsequently to contribute to the creation of a new martial art, eventually to be called judo, the gentle Way.

First, an imperial ordinance prohibiting the wearing of *samurai* swords was issued. This in effect signalled the swift degeneration of feudal-type martial arts schools which in some cases, despite extreme hardship, attempted to continue operations.

At about the same time an 11-year-old boy, Jigoro Kano, was taken by his family from his birth place of Mikage to live in Tokyo. Kano was physically an extremely small, weak child, who regularly experienced bullying from bigger schoolchildren. However, despite his diminutive physique, he refused to yield to these larger companions. In 1878, at the age of 18, as a highly capable student at Tokyo Imperial University, Kano investigated the possibility of studying *ju-jitsu*.

Owing to the social conditions at the time, Kano initially experienced great difficulty in locating a suitable teacher. However, being a tenacious individual, he eventually found an expert, Teinosuke Yagi, who taught him the rudiments of *ju-jitsu*. After diligent study Kano was introduced to masters Fakuda and Iso, who initiated him into the advanced secrets of their respective schools.

Despite many inhibiting circumstances, Kano eventually mastered *ju-jitsu* and became an acknowledged expert in his own right. At the same time, his academic career progressed and after graduating from university

Dr Kano was eventually appointed lecturer of political science and economics at the Peers School.

Whilst engaged in his study of *ju-jitsu* Dr Kano, being an academic, was able to identify the traumatic social and political transformation that was taking place in Japan as the country became more open to Western influences. It became obvious to him that the 'new' Japan could benefit greatly from the inclusion in the educational system of a traditional martial art-type activity. After extensive research Dr Kano eventually conceived the idea of adapting his *ju-jitsu* training as a means of physical and spiritual education. By eliminating the lethal techniques and adding some of his own inventions he formulated a new, scientific, educational martial art which was suitable for all ages.

To distinguish his art from *ju-jitsu*, Dr Kano created the name judo (meaning the gentle Way) and on the 5 June 1882, at the Eisho Temple, he formally opened the first judo establishment, which he named the *Kodokan* (the place where one practises the Way). On this auspicious occasion Dr Kano enjoyed the attendance of only one pupil who, according to the *Kodokan* register, was called T. Tomita.

Kodokan progress was slow but positive. The fact that Kano had retained the traditional *samurai* philosophy of honour, discipline and integrity, as well as courage, attracted many academics and people of noble birth. He regularly received requests from such individuals to cultivate the characters of their children through the principles and discipline of judo. Because of the academic and spiritual approach to his teachings, Kano was fortunate in that a number of skilled, traditional *ju-jitsu* experts identified the social and educational value of this 'new' martial art. They too became interested in judo, transferring their allegiance to Kano. Eventually, they became trusted assistants, some going on to be masters in their own right. Their names are legendary in judo circles today.

One such person was Shiro Saigo, an assistant

who had a habit of arriving late to take the class.

On one such occasion, Saigo found Dr Kano sitting in the centre of the *dojo* (place of practice) with a very solemn look on his face. Kano glanced at Saigo and, very quietly but firmly, said 'Why are you late? If no one is taking charge of the *dojo*, those who come here as pupils will go away. A *judoka* should have a strong sense of responsibility.' This was one of the many examples of what Kano was trying to achieve by his teaching of judo. From that moment on Saigo and other assistants were said to have been as punctual as the clock.

Despite many difficulties, the *Kodokan* progressed, gaining momentum each year. It became the centre of public attention, the high ideals appealing to academics and noble people throughout the country. However, apart from the normal administrative difficulties associated with pioneering projects, the *Kodokan* also found itself the victim of constant criticism. This arose from some old-guard *ju-jitsu* experts, who insisted that Kano's system had no practical merits in actual combat.

JU-JITSU VERSUS JUDO

During 1886 rivalry with these *ju-jitsu* schools reached a peak. Consequently, Kano found himself being forced to accept a challenge from one of the leading opponents responsible for the many criticisms levelled against the *Kodokan.*

This type of combat or challenge was completely contradictory to the way of *Kodokan* judo. However Kano had no choice — conditions in Japan were such that the police as well as the military authorities were showing an interest in unarmed combat training. More importantly, the education authorities were also becoming interested, with a view to including judo in the educational syllabus.

Realizing that his critics were desperately attempting to ease judo out of favour in an effort to re-establish the old-guard *ju-jitsu* schools, Kano accepted the challenge, and under the auspices of the Chief of the Tokyo Metropolitan

Police a grand tournament was arranged between the *Kodokan* and the *Totsuka* ju-jitsu school. This was indeed to be a decisive battle, involving 15 hand-picked contestants from both schools. Defeat would have been fatal for the *Kodokan*, its credibility destroyed, leading to total frustration of Kano's expansion plans.

The result of the tournament was incredible; even Kano must have been surprised at his overwhelming victory. Bout after bout produced victory for the *Kodokan*; in fact Kano and his team won all but two bouts, these being declared a draw. This brilliant victory established once and for all the supremacy of *Kodokan* judo, not only in principles but also in technique. Kano and the *Kodokan* were finally established, their future assured.

Shortly after this victory, the government granted official recognition to the *Kodokan*. This was followed by an improvement in relations with practitioners of *ju-jitsu*, some masters of the old guard transferring their allegiance to Kano. Judo became compulsory within the general education system, and Dr Kano was appointed as a special adviser to the Ministry of Education. This appointment was ultimately to aid the expansion of judo throughout the world.

20TH-CENTURY EXPANSION

The *Kodokan*'s progress accelerated and around the turn of the century, Dr Kano's travels extended to foreign countries, including Europe and in particular Britain. By now the *Kodokan* had new, larger premises and was vested with a constitutional body of 50 governors, with teachers spreading the art to a number of countries. Foreign visitors also began to trickle into the *Kodokan* for tuition, eventually returning to their home countries to begin teaching this new, fascinating art.

One would assume that by now *ju-jitsu* would have faded totally from the martial arts scene. This was not the case; in fact *ju-jitsu* preceded judo into Europe, with the arrival of Yukio Tani in London on the 26 September

1899. Subsequent years saw the arrival of a number of *ju-jitsu*/judo exponents who were eventually to contribute greatly to the development of European judo. Without the efforts of these experts, there is no telling how judo would have developed in the West. It is impossible to name every master who contributed to this expansion, but the names that spring to mind are Yukio Tani, Masutaro O-Tani, Gunji Koizumi, Kenshiro Abe, Hikoichi Aida, S.K. Uyenishi, Taro Miyake, Akitaro Ohno, Master Mifune, Minoru Mochizuki, Haku Michigami, and not forgetting, of course, Dr Jigoro Kano.

With the help of Japanese instructors, many clubs were opened in Europe. One establishment worthy of mention is the now-famous *Budokwai*, formed in London during the month of January 1918. Master Gunji Koizumi was primarily responsible for the development of the *Budokwai*, assisted by other Japanese experts including Dr Kano, who visited Britain a number of times during the early part of the 20th century.

Dr Kano continued travelling, his efforts between 1918 and 1938 resulting in worldwide expansion in numerous major countries. The *Kodokan* also welcomed foreign visitors to receive tuition at their Tokyo *dojo*, where there was a helpful exchange of judo techniques and ideology on an academic basis. In the West, sporting judo teams were formed, with contests arranged between various countries. For example, a German judo team visited Britain in 1930, and two years later an international summer school was formed, which was held each year until the outbreak of the Second World War.

Many Western practitioners can be remembered as being associated with the expansion of judo into Europe, all contributing in their own way to the development of the art in their respective countries, but one of the greatest European contributors to the growth of Western judo in the early 1930s was a British academic, Trevor Leggett.

In 1932 a young Trevor Leggett attended judo classes every night for approximately 15 months until he was finally awarded his black belt (first *dan*). This was an amazing achievement, especially as at the same time he was studying for a law degree at London University. Leggett's subsequent progress and technical ability, as well as his traditional approach, are well known in judo circles. In 1941, whilst serving in the British Embassy at Tokyo, he was able to train for several hours a day at the *Kodokan*, as well as visiting many local university clubs. During the war, despite being interned with other embassy staff, Leggett managed to practise with his Japanese guards. Being *judoka*, they respected the fact he had been graded by the *Kodokan* and was in fact senior in judo grade to several of those responsible for his security.

On his return to Britain after the war Leggett, along with many other European practitioners, continued to contribute to the worldwide expansion of judo. He became a respected, influential judo teacher, with personal high-level contacts at the *Kodokan*. At his club in London he insisted that all judo lessons be conducted in the Japanese language. This method of operation resulted in tremendous pressure by British *judoka* to anglicize the judo language, but Leggett continued to retain the traditional Japanese approach to training, so much so that he introduced the notorious 'special training' sessions. These included arduous, extended practice for days at a time, during the coldest and hottest days of the year. This method of martial arts training is famous in Japan. Students who successfully conclude these demanding training courses receive special certificates and are considered practitioners of repute.

At the conclusion of the Second World War, Leggett became head of the British Broadcasting Corporation's Japanese service. This enabled him to visit Japan regularly, where he was able to arrange for suitable European students to attend the *Kodokan*. Leggett would arrange for these special students not only to further their judo careers but also to learn the Japanese language. Like Dr Kano, Leggett was of the opinion that *judoka* should be associated with culture and education as well as sport. Furthermore Leggett arranged for many Japanese masters to visit Europe during the post-war years. All in all, Trevor Leggett is a man who should be remembered as one of the greatest non-Japanese pioneers of the gentle Way.

Meanwhile Dr Kano and his colleagues, dedicated to the expansion of the traditional martial art of judo, unselfishly gave their time and expertise to numerous countries — Britain, America, Canada, India, Germany, France, Egypt, Italy, Singapore, Hong Kong, New Zealand, Australia, South America, Afghanistan, Nepal. Circumstances affecting this worldwide expansion differed. In some cases experts authorized by Dr Kano to represent the *Kodokan* were dispatched to a country where they would reside for a time, teaching and educating selected national representatives in the traditional martial Way. Other methods included the opening of traditional judo clubs by suitably qualified individuals of the country concerned who had recognized the value of Dr Kano's system of character development.

An interesting contributor to Australian judo was Dr A.J. Ross who, at the age of nine, travelled with his parents to Japan, where he eventually attended the *Kodokan*. Ross qualified to the rank of black belt (first *dan*), then returned to Australia. After a period of displaying his judo skills in a travelling theatre company, he founded the Brisbane Judo Club and the Australian Judo Council in 1928. During 1948, Judo reached New Zealand when a Mr G. Grundy, a second *dan* black belt, arrived from Europe to open the Auckland Judo Club.

Many of these international judo pioneers are, unfortunately, no longer alive. However, one or two still enjoy good health and are able to act as sources of historical information to writers interested in this fascinating subject.

THE END OF AN ERA

The year 1938 is recognized by all traditional *judoka* as being the end of an era. On his return to Tokyo by ship, Dr Kano became ill and died unexpectedly, leaving his followers to continue his work.

Whilst the circumstances of Dr Kano's death were quite straightforward, it is interesting to note that he was at that time returning from Egypt, where he had been engaged in a meeting with the Olympic Committee. This might lead one to supppose that Dr Kano had decided to turn judo into an Olympic sport. However, in conversation with one of his followers, Master Mochizuki, Dr Kano described his reasons for the visit to Cairo. Kano at that time, completely independent of his judo activities, was a member of the Olympic Committee, his responsibility being to promote general sports in Japan and to represent Japan at this meeting. In Cairo there was never any discussion regarding the inclusion of judo in the Olympic Games. Kano's feelings on this point were made clear not only to Master Mochizuki, but also to European sportsman Baron Pierre De Coubertin. To these two individuals Dr Kano is alleged to have stated that it was impossible for judo to become an Olympic discipline, due to the fact it was not a sport. He then revealed his feelings to Baron Pierre De Coubertin: 'Everywhere in France you have a large number of churches, which are spiritual places. For me, Judo is like a church, it teaches a man a moral sense.' Kano is said to have explained to Baron De Coubertin and Master Mochizuki that competition in judo was not important. Sport was merely simple, physical exercise, whereas the aim of judo was completely different; he was adamant that his art included the search for an individual's personal development through the medium of physical combat exercises.

Dr Kano's loyal followers continued, after his death, to adopt his traditional teaching methods and philosophy. *Kodokan* representatives liaised with area organizations, stressing the character-building aspects of the gentle Way and the importance of regular practice. One of these representatives was Kyuzo Mifune, described as one of the greatest *judoka* of all time. Mifune joined the *Kodokan* in 1930, and after 10 years' training he achieved the grade of sixth *dan*, eventually becoming one of the senior *Kodokan* instructors. Mifune agreed with, and regularly practised, Kano's philosophy. He published a classic martial arts book, *Canon of Judo*, in which he described judo as follows: 'Judo is considered to be the combination of mental culture, physical training and feat of arms, all of which being used for self-perfection of human beings and their co-existence.'

By self-perfection, Master Mifune was explaining that the ultimate aim of judo training is primarily the development of one's character, and not the ability to win in combat. The student's sincerity and all-round effort towards this goal would eventually create a socially valuable person.

Whilst Mifune stressed the moral aspect of judo, there was no doubt that he was a fighter of tremendous skill. Although only small, weighing about 50 kg, Mifune once threw a 108 kg *sumo* wrestler. On another occasion, he found himself attacked by '13 rascals' in a restaurant, and in less than a minute dealt with seven of them. Like Kano, Mifune had studied, and mastered, the art almost to perfection, so much so that at the age of 70 he fought a young American major of the occupying forces to a standstill. When asked to describe the experience of fighting Mifune, a defeated opponent replied that it was like an elephant trying to throw a butterfly — there was no way strength and weight could dominate Master Mifune's skill and timing.

The year 1939 heralded the outbreak of the Second World War. Consequently, international judo activities slipped abruptly into decline, with many practitioners being called to the service of their respective countries.

POST-WAR YEARS

Immediately after the war an official ban applied by the occupying forces in Japan forbade the practising of all martial arts, and the resurgence of judo was greatly inhibited by this ordinance. However, because of the educational status of the *Kodokan*, judo appeared to experience an easier time than other fighting arts. Tuition was allowed to take place, and in fact many servicemen in occupation showed an interest in the art. Some of these practitioners were eventually to return to their respective countries to continue with their studies and contribute to international judo expansion.

The *Kodokan* rapidly regained its pre-war impetus and regularly received requests to dispatch instructors to various countries. Relationships with the West were renewed, and facilities at the *Kodokan* improved with the introduction of a special foreign section, as well as dormitories to accommodate residential students. It is now the Mecca of traditional judo, with an impressive multi-storey building housing an expansive mat area, with viewing facilities for spectators.

With the war fading into the past, the traditional exponents of Dr Kano's judo settled down to what they believed would be a stable, continued expansion of this fighting system of character development. However, they were completely unaware that sporting and political changes would result in a dramatic change of judo style and attitude.

The post-war years introduced to the international judo scene the formation of associations and federations, all attempting to formalize and/or control the expansion of this new and exciting activity — what they now referred to as a 'sport'. Expansion in Europe resulted in the formation of the European Judo Union (EJU), the British Judo Association (BJA) and other smaller organizations. But their interest in the traditional aspects of what they considered a martial art became secondary to the sporting element; the emphasis gradually switched to winning tournaments and medals. This approach to the art was completely contrary to Kano's creation, with many traditionalists and colleagues of Dr Kano becoming very concerned at the changes taking place. Fortunately, the East–West umbilical cord remained intact, so *Kodokan* experts were still able to teach the traditional way.

In 1964 judo was finally accepted as an official Olympic sport. By this time many national bodies were receiving financial support from their governments and sports councils. In return for this substantial financial assistance, judo teams found themselves in a position of having to deliver the goods, 'the goods' being contest successes and medals. It would be accurate to describe 1964 as the time when a change from traditional to sport judo took place. And with this change of direction came a definite decline in the quality of judo technique.

Despite this unfortunate change of attitude and direction, many skilful judo sportsmen acquired contest successes for their country. It is interesting to note that many of these individuals were weaned on the traditional teachings as advocated by Kano and the *Kodokan*. This demonstrated the effectiveness of *Kodokan* judo in sport-combat.

Kenshiro Abe

Kenshiro Abe, a brilliant *ju-jitsu* and judo expert of the old school, arrived in London during 1955. He became a highly respected and popular instructor, teaching his own particular style of traditional judo based on the development of the practitioner's character.

Abe was an unpredictable individualist, considered by some to be very eccentric. The truth was that Abe was nothing more than a highly-skilled *judoka* from a *samurai* background, dedicated to developing the character and spirit of his students. His attitude towards contest judo created considerable opposition, especially when he regularly reminded practitioners that it was not enough to win a contest at any cost. With the rapid expansion of sport judo, particularly towards Olympic recognition, Abe became a very unpopular instructor, but many traditionalists said that to reject such an expert's advice was a direct insult to the memory of Dr Kano.

To observe Abe practise his traditional style against the sporting champions of the day was an experience in itself. The very *judoka* criticizing this man were unable to avoid his dynamic throwing techniques, despite the fact Abe was middle-aged and his critics young, athletic types in their prime.

Gunji Koizumi

Known as the father of European judo, Gunji Koizumi influenced the judo scene in Europe more than any other instructor. Like Dr Kano, Koizumi enjoyed a *samurai* background and was a highly skilful practitioner, as well as being a gentleman and a scholar.

After a number of short visits to Europe and America, Koizumi eventually chose Britain as his headquarters, from where he contributed to the expansion of judo in England, Austria, Germany, Switzerland and America. Being an academic gentleman, Master Koizumi shared Dr Kano's attitude to martial arts training, and he strove to inject the traditional attitudes into judo students in a style that was completely compatible with the way of Kano and the *Kodokan.*

Sadly, on the 15 April 1965, a year after the official acknowledgment of judo as an Olympic sport, Gunji Koizumi died in true *samurai* style — by committing suicide. The circumstances surrounding the death of Master Koizumi remain a secret to this day, but it is known that prior to his death he dispatched a letter to his superiors in Japan, informing them of his intention and voicing his dissatisfaction at the decline in judo standards.

Masutaro O-Tani

From 1919 until his death in 1977 Masutaro O-Tani loyally spread the traditional style of judo throughout various areas of Europe. From his headquarters in London he assisted in the operation of the British Judo

Council (BJC), once controlled by Kenshiro Abe. O-Tani was an extremely modest man who, dedicated to the traditional way, managed to continue practising until a very advanced age. He was totally uninfluenced by the introduction of judo into the Olympics, and simply continued with his own approach to the art.

FUTURE OF JUDO

With the passing away of these traditional masters, an obvious question to be asked is what will happen in the future?

With the almost overwhelming expansion of judo it is quite clear that the sporting version of Dr Kano's art is here to stay. International organizations will continue to receive financial support from governments and sports councils, with the number one priority being to win medals. The character-building and spiritual aspects of traditional judo will be shelved in favour of contest tricks.

Fortunately, the *Kodokan* remains as the Mecca of the gentle Way, and with small groups of dedicated practitioners seeking to retain the qualities of the art it is hoped that new apprentices will be encouraged to undertake traditional tuition. In addition to the *Kodokan*, modern practitioners of the traditional martial arts, including judo, are able to refer to the *Dai Nippon Butoku Kai*, Japan's great Martial Virtues Association. Formed in April 1895, the *Dai Nippon Butoku Kai* was sanctioned by the government to control and standardize the various martial arts in Japan. A great debt of gratitude is owed to this traditional organization whose origins can be traced back as far as Emperor Kanmu (781-805 AD). Respect, compassion, gratitude, integrity and honour are the virtues of this age-old institute, whose activities are primarily directed towards maintaining traditional standards in all Japanese martial arts. An example of the *Dai Nippon Butoku Kai*'s contribution to this task was the formation of the Martial Arts Technical College.

The Association stresses the importance of traditional

martial arts training for all in the general education system, and includes a comprehensive study of the code of the *samurai* warrior in its syllabus. In addition to tuition in the fighting arts of Japan, the Association also operates a two- and four-year graduate programme in a number of academic subjects. Graduates of this élite academy are often referred to as Japan's most highly-educated and skilled martial arts experts.

Despite the worldwide sporting approach of judo, the traditional *samurai* approach to life and martial arts will never become obsolete as long as organizations such as the *Kodokan* and the *Dai Nippon Butoku Kai* continue to operate. Western governments could well benefit from examining both the Japanese educational system, and how Eastern society adopts a *bushido* style of discipline in their everyday lives. The result is a very low crime rate and an extremely successful business community.

2
GETTING STARTED

BEFORE YOU START

Clothing and equipment

Unlike many sporting activities, judo requires special clothing in the form of hard-wearing white jacket, trousers and belt. Tracksuits are sometimes allowed, but quite honestly are not advisable because the student can only engage in warming-up exercises and *ukemi* (breakfalls). So a judo suit is essential from the start. Most sports retailers sell judo suits (referred to in judo circles as a *judo-gi*), costs varying from £20 to £70 (1989 prices) depending on the quality, size and manufacturer. Sizes range from 120 cm to 200 cm (small, medium and large i.e. approximately 4 feet to 6 feet 6 inches). Occasionally it is possible for students to acquire their *judo-gi* on loan from clubs. For women and girls a T-shirt worn under the jacket is essential, as the jacket can very easily flop open. It is also advisable to wear a good bra or a sports bra.

It would also be useful to acquire a simple pair of slippers or sandals for general movement between the changing rooms and mat area. Surprisingly, experienced *judoka* are occasionally seen wandering round club premises in bare feet — this is not recommended as it is unhygienic.

Personal hygiene

This is a very important aspect of a judo student's preparation. You will be coming into close physical contact with other people, and there is nothing more unpleasant than practising with a partner who has long toenails or fingernails, or who smells. Obviously, any open wounds should be covered with a suitable dressing. Jewellery is forbidden.

Personal hygiene is nothing more than commonsense, but despite this it is surprising how many practitioners bleed on their partners or cause injury with dangerously long nails. To ensure good hygiene you should have a clean white suit (*judo-gi*), a clean body and teeth, short toe/fingernails, and no jewellery. You should also wash your feet before entering the mat area, and cover all open wounds, scabs, etc.

Useful items in a student's sports bag are plenty of plasters and small bandages, plus a bar of soap and a toothbrush and paste.

Age

A person's age should not affect their decision to study a martial art. A well-known example of an older person commencing judo from scratch is Dr John B. Hanson-Lowe. At 51 years of age this amazing individual decided to give judo a try. In 1960 he retired from work as a geologist with an international oil company and travelled to Japan, where he embarked on a six months' training programme at the *Kodokan*. Dr Hanson-Lowe eventually decided to settle in Japan, where now, at the age of 79, he enjoys the rank of *Kodokan* fourth *dan* (black belt), and still practises regularly. His academic, scientific approach to the art has enabled him to continue until this advanced age.

Judo is for everyone and, providing a potential student can locate a suitable traditional club, there will always be a place for people of all ages, male or female, interested in studying this fascinating martial art.

Children

A sensible minimum starting age for children is seven. Younger children are less able to concentrate, and this could have serious repercussions during a lesson. And parents considering judo for the younger members of their family should apply the commonsense rules regarding medical conditions.

Physical condition

Whilst age should not affect an individual's decision to study judo, consideration must be given to one's current physical condition before embarking on a period of training. Generally fit individuals will cope with the overall physical exertions involved, but obese or unfit people could experience problems if they neglect to adopt commonsense precautions. No matter what age, grossly overweight men and women employed in sedentary professions will find their introduction to judo an uncomfortable reminder of just how unfit they are, especially if they are generally unfamiliar with exercise. Depending on their social habits, i.e. drinking, smoking, overeating, late nights, etc., the effects of training could be most unpleasant, or even dangerous. This does not mean potential *judoka* should decide against taking up judo; on the contrary, a more determined approach should be adopted.

A good way to start would be to have a few early nights, accompanied by a review of eating (see pages 68-69) and drinking habits, followed by a gradual change to a more sensible lifestyle. Gentle stretching exercises, walking, or even jogging, are excellent methods of preparing the body for training in martial arts.

Anyone suffering a medical condition should not embark on a course of judo training without consulting with their doctor. It would also be prudent to inform the intended instructor about any medical problems that might cause difficulties, for example if you are diabetic. Generally speaking, most teachers will be only too pleased to encourage and assist individuals suffering from any disorder, including blindness, deafness or physical disability. (See pages 93-94.)

FINDING A CLUB AND INSTRUCTOR

Ideally, a budding *judoka* should decide early on what
they are hoping to achieve from a study of the gentle Way.
The best method of dealing with this consideration is to
pose the following questions:

- Do I simply want to keep fit and learn self defence?
- Do I want to engage in judo competitions with a
  possibility of reaching a high competitive level?
- Do I hope to benefit in other ways, such as personal
  development, character building, etc?

Having answered these questions, the next and most
important task is to locate a suitable club. A first
experience could well be the last in the hands of an
unorthodox instructor.

So before setting out to find a club a potential student
should decide whether to follow a sporting or traditional
system of judo training. This will depend entirely on the
personality of the budding apprentice, their age and
circumstances. Whatever the verdict, though, in the
interests of safety and quality of instruction, the following
steps are recommended:

- Contact the official organization controlling judo in the
  resident country. Acquire a list of clubs, with details of
  instructors' qualifications.
- Shortlist a number of potential clubs, arrange a visit
  and a discussion with the chief instructor.
- Visit the club, assess the instructor's attitude, as well
  as the general facilities.
- Arrange to watch a lesson involving low grade *judoka*.
  Analyse the instructor's disposition and method of
  operation.

A professionally-operated club will be clean and tidy, with
suitable changing rooms plus toilet facilities, both for male
and female members. The mat area will be large enough to
accommodate safely a suitable number of students who

may be practising at any one time. Only approved judo mats, surrounded by a safety zone, should be in use.

'No smoking' signs should be displayed throughout the club, this rule being religiously obeyed by all members, especially the instructor. An informative club noticeboard, displaying practice times divided between adults and children, depending on their grade, special events, etc., is a useful item. First aid facilities are essential, including a medical supplies box, and a quiet area where an injured student can be treated. A telephone is vital.

Permeating the club should be a relaxed, friendly atmosphere, with low-grade *judoka* showing respect for their seniors, but at the same time these seniors adopting a respectful attitude towards the lower grades, particularly during the actual training session. Classes should be conducted with an air of calm discipline, with the instructor showing total control over his students. The actual lesson should be constructed in the following manner:

- All students should line up and bow to the instructor prior to the commencement of the lesson.
- General warming-up exercises should be conducted by either the senior grade or the instructor in charge.
- *Ukemi* (art of breakfalling) exercises are essential to safe, progressive judo and should be included in every lesson.
- At this stage, depending on the instructor's lesson plan, actual judo technique will be demonstrated, followed by student practice.
- Special attention should be paid to the lowest-graded members of the class.

Bad indications

To a reasonably intelligent person an unsuitable club will be very obvious. The following observations at a particular club should encourage all potential students to seek alternative instruction:

- Dirty premises.
- Lack of suitable changing room facilities.
- An untidy and/or unhelpful instructor who tends to exaggerate the quality of his students' and club's successes.
- Uneven or damaged mat area.
- Lack of first aid facilities, especially a telephone.
- Lack of general discipline, smoking in the *dojo* and disrespect between club members.
- An instructor who does not appear to have a constructive lesson plan.
- Any instructor teaching unusual and/or dangerous judo techniques should be avoided at all costs.
- Any club where participants engage in wrestling-style techniques.

Under no circumstances should a potential student attend a club where the instructor is in the habit of relinquishing control or supervision over the students — it is very dangerous to leave inexperienced pupils to their own devices. In certain Western clubs this is a regular occurrence, and has resulted in serious accidents. Depending on the circumstances, it might well be acceptable to appoint a senior grade to supervise for a short period, but generally an instructor should be present and remain in total control throughout the lesson.

Instructors

An important point to note relates to the experience and qualifications of a *judoka* wearing a black belt, as this does not automatically qualify the wearer as a judo coach. There are a number of Western black belt holders who have achieved sporting titles via the use of very unorthodox judo techniques, even though their basic traditional knowledge of the art is quite often limited. Such practitioners tend to apply their own particular style to their teaching which, in some cases, is very dangerous.

To check the credentials of an instructor is not an easy

task for the nervous student. However, a discussion with the parent organization responsible for the control of judo should reveal details of the actual coaching qualifications held. Most authorities operate special schemes for the training of coaches, and certificates or licences are normally held by suitably qualified tutors. It could be that a certificate will be displayed on the club noticeboard, in which case details can be noted, followed by enquiries with the controlling body to confirm validity.

However, a club dedicating its activities purely to sport judo should not necessarily be considered unsuitable. There are numerous clubs all over the world interested only in the tournament side of the art, but that manage to maintain basic traditional discipline as well as character development. Usually, such clubs are controlled by instructors trained in the traditional way who have simply directed their efforts into competitive sport. There are certain clubs, though, that have abandoned very important basics, such as *ukemi* (the art of falling), as well as other aspects of discipline. This type of club should be avoided as their contribution to the art is minimal, and such an establishment usually has a very high accident rate.

Costs of joining a club

In addition to purchasing a judo suit, practitioners will find it necessary to pay subscription fees annually to their parent club. There will also normally be a regular charge each session and when gradings are taken. Most controlling organizations also have an annual charge for the judo licence, which is required by all practitioners.

Costs vary, depending on the country and professional organizations. In the United Kingdom the annual cost can be broken-down as follows:—

Club membership	£10-£30 per annum
Purchase of suit	£20-£50
Licence	£14 per annum
Practice fees	£1-£4 per session
Grading	£3-£6 per grading

HOW TO BEGIN

Having chosen a suitable club, the potential student has one final decision to make. There are two methods of embarking on a judo training programme, from which the enthusiast must choose:

- Throwing themselves in at the deep end and simply joining in a class, picking it up gradually over a number of weeks.
- Undertaking a special beginners' course of something like 12 weeks' duration.

Joining in

To a certain extent this can be a reasonably satisfactory method of learning judo. However, unless a second instructor is available to act as a 'shepherd' to the beginner, it is quite possible that certain (very important) basic elements will be omitted. This system of training is quite popular with some Western clubs and, providing the apprentice is supervised by the additional instructor and that breakfalling (*ukemi*) is not neglected, then this approach to learning is acceptable.

Basic course

This is by far the most suitable method of learning any kind of physical activity, especially a martial art. Such courses are usually constructed in such a way that maximum progress is achieved in the time involved, which is usually about 12 weeks, divided into a minimum of two lessons a week.

A basic course will include a general introduction to the history of judo, more than likely accompanied by printed matter designed to assist the student in understanding exactly how the course will progress. At the conclusion of the course it is possible that a grading test will be conducted by the instructor, who might be authorized by the controlling body to conduct such examinations.

Sharing the trials and tribulations of any basic physical

training programme with fellow students is usually quite exciting, and often results in rapid development of an individual's character. In addition, the technical aspects of basic training are usually more quickly assimilated than during a 'joining in' lesson. All in all, the basic course is highly recommended.

Psychological preparation

Having acquired the necessary equipment and decided on the method of training, the student's first feelings of trepidation will occur. Throughout the day prior to the first lesson a general feeling of nervousness may be experienced. This is quite normal, so the recruit should not dwell on such emotions.

However, it is very important that a certain mental attitude is created prior to the lesson. This enables the student to relax, which is essential if progress is to be achieved. The following recommendations will assist the student in the mental preparation for a first lesson:

- Avoid a heavy meal before training.
- Avoid any form of alcohol for several hours prior to training.
- Arrive at the club with at least 30 minutes to spare prior to the lesson.
- Report to the instructor at the appointed time, in a clean and tidy condition. Under no circumstances should a student be late for any lesson.

WHAT TO EXPECT

Depending on the instructor, general methods of operation may vary. However, despite whatever personal approaches to tuition are adopted, there are certain basic elements that should be included. It is vital to the retention of traditional practice that these aspects of judo are included in every lesson.

Prior to actual tuition, students will be expected to stand in a straight line and then, from a kneeling position, bow to the instructor. There will then follow a brief period of warming-up exercises. This introduction to a traditional lesson is standard practice, and the warming-up period should last about 15 minutes.

Dojo (place of practising the Way) discipline should be familiar to the enthusiastic student, who by now will possibly have watched a lesson or acquired a leaflet describing the various rules and regulations of the club. Alternatively, the instructor or senior member may have discussed these points.

Kneeling position

Standing position

Methods of bowing.

Sensei

This is a most important Japanese word that should be
learned and understood prior to the first lesson. *Sensei*
simply means teacher or instructor. In traditional circles,
all pupils should address their instructor by this title.

The lesson itself

Following the period of limbering-up exercises, the
instructor will demonstrate the art of breakfalling or
ukemi. In a beginners' class *ukemi* practice could last for
the whole of the first lesson. Students should appreciate
that skilful judo cannot be developed without the ability
to fall correctly.

The art of *ukemi* is unique to judo and is, without
doubt, the most important aspect of training. It is not in
itself a technique, but a special method of falling that can
be adopted when being thrown to the mat by someone else
in the class or by an enemy in real-life combat.

Many Western practitioners engaged in sport judo have
a habit of ignoring breakfalls, their philosophy being that
to fall is to be beaten. This attitude leads to incorrect
practice, and is extremely dangerous to both parties.
Without the ability to fall correctly, participants
tend to hang on to their partners when being thrown. If
they do this, injury can occur because the person hanging
on is unable to execute a correct breakfall anyway, and,
invariably, the thrower is pulled down on top of the faller,
possibly resulting in a broken rib, damaged shoulder or
neck, or even a serious back injury. Also by hanging on,
the offender sometimes causes a collision of heads, which
again may cause serious injury to both participants.

Mastering *ukemi* should be every student's number one
priority. The ability to fall correctly cannot be over-
stressed — it can mean the difference between a fatal
injury or simply getting up and walking away from a
violent fall.

As soon as the instructor observes an understanding of
breakfalling, students will then be introduced to the
method of gripping and a basic throw, although it is highly

unlikely that throwing techniques will be taught during the first lesson.

A beginner's first lesson should last about 1 hour 30 minutes, including warming up exercises and *ukemi* practice. To conclude, a period of 'warming down' exercises should then be carried out, following which all students will again line up to make a kneeling bow to their teacher. It is advisable after any martial arts lesson to enjoy a shower, followed by a period of relaxation accompanied by non-alcoholic refreshment. *Kuchi-wazi* (talking) sessions can be an interesting part of general development.

CLUB DISCIPLINE AND ETIQUETTE

Traditional judo training must include the strict code of discipline and etiquette, as created and practised by the *samurai* warriors of Japan. Without these formalities, whatever is being practised is not a martial art but simply a method of fighting. There are many individuals, studying Oriental systems of combat safely and successfully, who don't consciously adopt anything more than commonsense and respect for their colleagues. Such practitioners contribute to society and have reached very high levels in their *budo* training, but it is also obvious that they have subconsciously adopted aspects of the *samurai* code. Adopting the *samurai* code comprehensively is by far the best method for the individual who wishes to cope with the trials and tribulations of modern society. Self discipline, commonsense and self control in fraught situations are qualities which are developed by the dedicated martial artist. With regular practice in the traditional Way, all *judoka* should be able to extend their new-found attributes to everyday life.

To many Westerners this code of conduct may be initially embarrassing or difficult to adopt. However, serious followers quickly settle down to this system, and it is refreshing in modern society to observe groups of individuals adopting such respect for each other.

Some Western *judoka* have criticized this Oriental system of respect for others, insisting that such conduct is outdated and inappropriate to Western society. Those critics should examine Eastern society, and then perhaps they will realize how the Japanese, being an immensely practical race, have achieved tremendous social and commercial success. The rituals that exist are not simply carried out for decorative reasons. Experienced practitioners of any martial art — judo, *karate*, *aikido*, *kendo* — all appreciate the benefits of adopting the *samurai* code of conduct, and the benefits to be derived from it.

One good Western example of *dojo* etiquette is that adopted by the Eurokwai Judo and Karate Club in Britain. Most clubs throughout the world follow a similar though, not necessarily identical, system.

- Bow on entering or leaving the *dojo*.
- Bow to all partners during training.
- Address all instructors as *sensei*.
- Do not leave the class without the instructor's permission.
- Late arrivals must adopt a kneeling position on the edge of the mat and await the instructor's permission to join the class.
- Fingernails and toenails must be kept short and clean.
- No wearing of jewellery.
- Refrain from swearing or smoking in the *dojo*.
- Members must not commit any act that will offend the etiquette of the *dojo*.
- Senior grades are to respect lower grades.
- Refrain from impetuous or violent behaviour, in or out of the *dojo*.
- No alcohol before the lesson.

In some Western martial arts clubs a few undisciplined members regularly conduct themselves in a most unattractive manner. Incidents involving swearing, unnecessary violence directed to lower grades, as well as actual fighting in the streets, all serve to remind traditionalists that self-discipline and orderly conduct are vital to a peaceful, progressive society. These individuals are not true, committed *judoka*.

PROGRESS

Two factors will affect a student's progress: the attitude and ability of the instructor and the seriousness and enthusiasm of the trainee. If both parties adopt a suitable approach to the art, it is inevitable that a spiritual, progressive bond will develop between them which will have a beneficial effect on the student's progress. This teacher–pupil relationship can quite easily last for many years.

Throughout the early lessons the instructor will, as soon as breakfalls are performed safely, introduce his pupils to throwing techniques, holds and grappling on the ground. In addition, depending on the age of pupils, strangles and armlocks will be briefly examined. All in all, a beginners' course will be quite basic and designed in such a manner that participants will progress through breakfalling to general throwing techniques. On its conclusion, there should be little or no difficulty in executing a correct fall whilst being thrown by a partner. These weeks of basic training will also encourage students to appreciate general fitness, as well as the necessity for discipline and etiquette.

One important point that should be stressed by instructors is the fact that the actual execution of judo techniques does not rely on strength. Continuous reference should be made for the need physically to relax the arms. There are many ways of demonstrating this relaxed style and instructors with a traditional grounding in the art have their own methods of teaching this. Accentuating the negative use of physical strength as a requirement for the practice of judo cannot be over-stressed. It is vital that all *judoka*, beginners as well as advanced practitioners, regularly remind themselves there is no necessity for brute strength and resistance — the key to success is to 'bend like the willow'.

GRADINGS AND PROMOTION

Having concluded the basic course, students are either fired with enthusiasm or fall by the wayside. In a Western class of, say, 30 starters it is not uncommon for less than half to complete the course. Experienced instructors quickly identify the genuine types who display potential dedication and ability. Despite being clumsy, or perhaps physically incapable of initially performing a technique, participants who are obviously trying their best and who display the right attitude will receive appropriate encouragement from their instructor. The less dedicated person, who may well be physically capable, will receive 'corrective tuition'. If there is no response and there remains an 'attitude problem', the answer is simple. They are encouraged to leave. There is no room for conceit or laziness in a judo club.

For the remainder a natural and exciting extension of the basic course is a grading examination. This usually takes place every three months and is considered by many *judoka* as quite an ordeal. In reality, it is nothing more than a test of the applicant's technical knowledge and their ability to fight under formal, controlled combat conditions. Gradings involve the following:

- Demonstration of named techniques given to students in Japanese.
- Two or three contests where the student is expected to win!
- *Kata* for first *dan* grading and above.
- For first *dan* and above, some countries have an interview system and candidates are expected to submit an essay.

As long as the correct mental attitude has been applied throughout training, the occasion of a grading should not be a problem. Promotion in judo is not something the practitioner should worry about. What will be, will be. The number one priority should be concentration on dedicated, regular study of the art.

Worldwide grading systems vary, but do have much in common. For instance, in most countries these examinations are conducted by authorized representatives of the organizations controlling judo. This affects the candidate, in that it will be necessary to obtain an official licence and record book. At the conclusion of the examination the record book is marked with evidence of the practitioner's grade, and sometimes a certificate is awarded to successful candidates.

The main similarity between the different grading systems is in the colour of belts worn by *judoka*. A general system of judo status is as shown in the accompanying table.

Judo grading system

Rank	Colour of belt	Approximate length of time at grade
Beginner	White	3 months
9th *kyu*	Yellow	3 months
8th *kyu*	Orange	3 months
7th *kyu*	Orange	3 months
6th *kyu*	Green	3 months
5th *kyu*	Green	3 months
4th *kyu*	Blue	3 months
3rd *kyu*	Blue	3 months
2nd *kyu*	Brown	3 months
1st *kyu*	Brown	3 months
1st *dan*	Black	6 months

Having reached the rank of black belt, further promotion through the *dan* grades can be achieved after protracted and diligent study. In certain Western judo circles, success in competition can be a contribution to advanced promotion. This is a most unsatisfactory method, resulting in a number of high grade *judoka* lacking in certain technical knowledge and ability normally associated with advanced grades. Martial artists who have qualified in the traditional methods, however, invariably possess this knowledge and experience.

A grading examination should not be an occasion where the practitioner is concerned about winning or losing his bout. It represents many things, and is not to be considered as a fight — judo purists treat these occasions as anything but. The following descriptions by various traditional practitioners who have engaged in grading examinations for a number of years illustrate this:

- A struggle for survival.
- A struggle for perfection.
- An occasion to improve.
- An opportunity to identify weakness.
- An opportunity to face and conquer fear.

A constructive way of approaching a grading examination is to consider the whole event a competition against oneself, an opportunity to test personal limitations. To abandon the idea of winning at all costs and to simply extend one's personal threshold can be an exhilarating experience that can create an abundance of confidence in the most insecure of people. Any *judoka* who simply treats a grading examination as an opportunity to improve rank by 'beating' other candidates is definitely travelling along a very short path.

INJURIES

Most physical pursuits have injuries peculiar to them. Martial arts, by their very nature, attract certain injuries, mainly caused by negligence or misconduct. In any sport or physical activity, the conduct of the participant is bound to affect the number of injuries sustained. There are also a number of general wear and tear problems that cannot be avoided.

Traditional judo clubs are generally very disciplined, the result being that serious injuries are few and far between, while the less serious problems invariably heal in a very short time, and usually involve ankles, legs, backs and sometimes elbows. However the activities of clubs involved in sport judo are such that it is not uncommon for one club to experience a number of serious accidents throughout the year, many of these injuries involving players holding area or national fighter status. The main cause of such sporting accidents is the unorthodox stance or style of the combatants, accompanied by their habit of refusing to execute a correct breakfall.

What is worse is that a number of Western clubs involved primarily in tournament judo appear to lack even basic discipline. At one very famous European club a well-known competitor was observed head-butting his partner in the stomach, while at the same club black belts were seen bullying low grades. This type of conduct is dangerous, and is akin to street brawling. It is also a complete distortion of the art of judo.

All judo instructors are responsible for the welfare of their pupils. To ensure maximum safety most controlling authorities insist that their coaches are experienced in first aid. Certain teachers from the traditional school may also be experienced in the ancient art of *katsu*. Students who enjoy the skills of an instructor capable of controlling members and who is qualified in first aid or experienced in *katsu*, in a club with good-quality mats, supported by suitable medical facilities, should have little or no worries about their safety.

Katsu

Again the *samurai* warriors of old are to be congratulated on their skills, this time with regard to resuscitation. For years, these élite warriors utilized certain delicate pressure points of the body for the purpose of rendering opponents unconscious or even dead. But these same pressure points were eventually discovered as being invaluable in the resuscitation of unconscious colleagues. For many years *katsu* was taught and practised by traditional Eastern martial arts masters, who usually imparted the secrets of the system only to trusted, advanced students.

This unusual method of resuscitation is not normally practised in the West. However, certain instructors have acquired the knowledge, which is an invaluable contribution to *dojo* safety. In many Japanese clubs *katsu* is included in advanced training. It is usually demonstrated by the instructor, who simply renders a student insensible with either a blow to the neck or a strangle technique. This is followed by a speedy manipulation of a specific pressure point, bringing the victim back to normal. Such demonstrations are very impressive, and create tremendous confidence in the ability of the tutor.

3
PHILOSOPHY AND BENEFITS OF JUDO

WHAT IS JUDO?

There have been many Western attempts to describe the essence of judo accurately. Most people have been able to understand the translation, 'gentle Way', but to elaborate further has usually resulted in a misunderstanding of the fundamental philosophy of the art. Such distortion is invariably due to the fact that Western practitioners come from a different culture and are unfamiliar with the Eastern attitudes to life. And it is impossible for novices to comprehend the philosophy behind any activity or art before they have personally experienced lengthy study and practice. To ask them for a description, would be akin to asking a traveller to describe a journey not yet commenced.

The early stages of study are very important to the judo student. If no attempt is made to steer the individual's attitude in the direction of character development, the result will more than likely be a semi-proficient *judoka* with no understanding of what the art is all about. However, students can help themselves by referring to publications written by the various masters. Over the years, there have been many attempts by judo masters to educate the Western mind in the philosophy of the art. These works have been profound and informative, and consequently many non-Japanese *judoka* have gained an insight to the true Way.

In 1957 senior *Kodokan* instructor Master Shinzo

Takagaki offered this interpretation of the objectives of judo:

> In a narrow sense, judo can be defined as the study of the maximum use of the body and mind for the purpose of attack and defence. In a wider sense, the principles of judo can be applied to all affairs of life. The ultimate object of judo is the perfection of oneself by the systematic training of the mind and body through exercise so that each works in harmony with the other.

This concise but informative piece should prove very useful to the novice. And Jigoro Kano, the founder of judo, should not be overlooked; in particular a study should be made of his in-depth explanation:

> The principle of the maximum, efficient use of mind and body is the fundamental principle governing all the techniques of judo. But it is also something more. The same principle can be applied to the improvement of the human body, making it strong, healthy and useful, and so constitute physical education. It can also be applied to the improvement of intellectual and moral power and in this way constitute mental and moral education. It can be applied to the improvement of diet, clothing, housing, social intercourse and methods of business, thus constituting a study of living.

The personal philosophy of Kenshiro Abe is hidden in the words *Kyu-shin-do*. A loose translation of this code of conduct is 'The seeker's way to the essence of things, or the truth.' Abe's philosophical approach to judo was similar to that of other Japanese maters, with one or two scientific differences. Three fundamental principles that he injected into his teaching were:

- That all things throughout the universe are in a constant state of motion.
- This motion is rhythmic and flowing.
- All things work and flow in perfect harmony.

Kenshiro Abe's personal *dojo* code was:

> Politeness, rules of behaviour and common decency are
> very much a part of judo. All Judoka are expected to
> acquaint themselves with this etiquette. After starting
> judo practice, one should never give up, but continue
> with a strong mind determined to overcome difficulties.

The road to understanding is long, and paved with
disappointments, frustrations, failures, and possibly a
little success. However, being determined to try again,
despite setbacks is all part of a *judoka*'s spiritual training.
It is often said that to reach the rank of black belt is
nothing more than completing induction, with the main
task or journey about to commence. To understand every
facet of any martial art is as impossible as understanding
life, but as long as the practitioner can appreciate that
judo is not primarily a fighting sport, but a method of
developing one's character, of confronting oneself and
life's problems, then this is a step in the right direction.

JU — GENTLE

One useful method of appreciating certain aspects of judo
is to study and understand the principle of *ju*. It is not
enough to simply know that *ju* means 'gentle'; a deeper
understanding is required.

Dr Kano instructed his students to forget any form of
resistance, but to flow with the general movement of
things. This not only applies physically in a judo practice,
but also in life, whether social or professional.

An example of non-resistance in judo practice might be
when a small practitioner is pushed by a larger, much
stronger partner. The smaller person, by adopting the
principle of non-resistance, moves with his partner in a
totally relaxed fashion. This results in the stronger person
becoming unstable, the weaker partner then taking
advantage of this unstable condition executes a
combat technique.

As an example of non-resistance in a social or business environment, let us imagine two people engaged in hectic negotiations or discussions. One individual is physically stronger, attempting to dominate the weaker person professionally or socially. By adopting the principle of non-resistance, the weak person can bide their time and eventually take advantage of the stronger person's compromised circumstances. By employing the system of *ju*, the weaker person is transformed into the stronger person.

This is an essentially *samurai* method of operation, and it dominates Japanese society, especially the business fraternity. It is extremely successful, especially when accompanied by a disciplined code of ethics and respect for others. The state of 20th century Japan is culture and economic progress is an excellent indication of what can be achieved by this *samurai* attitude to life.

ZEN AND JUDO

Zen is a subject that requires dedicated and protracted study. Briefly, Zen philosophy appears to have originated in 12th century China. It teaches the contemplation of an individual's essential nature to the exclusion of everything else, and is a way of achieving pure enlightenment.

The late Taisen Deshimaru was born in Japan of an old *samurai* family. His writings on Zen and the martial arts are an invaluable reference to traditional *judoka*. He describes the unbreakable connection between Zen, martial arts and the *samurai*. Zen has been part of *samurai* culture as long as the *samurai* have existed. It is described as many things, including 'True profound sound silence', and has also been translated as objectless concentration or meditation. On occasions it has been referred to as 'The original pure human spirit'.

According to Master Deshimaru, despite the academic moral approach that one should adopt in training and life, the attitude to actual combat is expected to be positive, with total commitment. Fear of defeat, or even death, should not exist. The following statements from Master Deshimaru transmit in crystal-clear terminology the state of mind that should exist permanently within all practising martial artists:

- 'You must concentrate upon and consecrate yourself wholly to each day, as though a fire were raging in your hair.'
- 'In the spirit of Zen and judo, everyday life becomes the contest. There must be awareness at every moment — getting up in the morning, working, eating, going to bed. That is the place for the mastery of self.'
- 'I have nothing against sports, they train the body, develop stamina and endurance. But the spirit of competition and power that presides over them is not good. It reflects a distorted vision of life. The root of the martial arts is not there.'

PHYSICAL FITNESS

A prolonged life — this should be the aim of every practising *judoka*. By persevering in serious training in the traditional style, this will be achieved, but longevity requires daily all-round consideration of one's lifestyle.

It is surprising how many people abuse their bodies throughout the week, then at weekends stumble around a golf course or squash court, actually believing they are physically fit. In fact, this continuous abuse, accompanied by strenuous exercise, can in certain cases be most unhealthy for the negligent individual. The human body requires regular servicing in the form of all-round stimulation, suitable food, as well as rest and recuperation. Training in traditional martial arts, especially judo, develops the mind of the practitioner in such a way that this care and attention becomes an everyday routine.

All judo students reach different levels of physical fitness. Obviously a beginner with only two weeks' experience enjoys a lot less fitness than the advanced black belt. For example at the conclusion of a basic course (about three months), a minimal degree of fitness will be attained in these early stages of development. The practitioner will enjoy the ability to complete a number of physical exercises, as well as a reasonably strenuous 90-minute lesson. The instructor's gradual augmentation of physical activity should no longer be a problem for the student. At this stage budding adepts should also be showing an interest in their body, as well as general considerations that create all-round health.

As training progresses (after about six months), exciting changes occur in the body. Loss of weight is usually experienced, as well as a general tightening and toning of muscles. Students also find it possible to exert themselves in general activities. An interest in the body's requirements should now have a permanent place in the practitioner's daily life. Usually around this intermediate stage of training, curiosity develops as regards dietary requirements and damage caused through alcohol and smoking.

For the dedicated trainee (after about 12 months) there are numerous rewards that can be gained. Regular practice for one year does not, however, create a black belt. On the contrary, the judo grade achieved in this period will normally only be the rank of sixth *kyu*. Nevertheless, the degree of physical fitness cultivated can be quite extraordinary. With a dedicated, constructive study of the art, the practitioner will have reached an extremely high standard of physical fitness. Excess weight will have disappeared, and he or she will have gained prolonged stamina and the ability to function under pressure for long periods. Judo also develops and enhances co-ordination, balance, speed and reflexes. It has been known for students to completely change their lifestyle by this stage in training. There are many examples of individuals who have commenced judo as weak, unfit addicts of junk food and alcohol, to be transformed into super-fit, highly capable athletes.

General all-round fitness will only be achieved with

dedication to correct judo procedures, accompanied by a sensible lifestyle outside the *dojo*. The necessity for eating good, nutritious food has never been so urgent as in the present day (see pages 68-69). Junk food, as well as alcohol, have invaded society, and consequently individuals of all ages have experienced a serious decline in health. This should not be so for a *judoka*.

Once an advanced stage of physical fitness has been reached the dedicated student will slowly become aware of additional changes in demeanour. These mental and physical improvements will differ, depending on the degree of fitness and the lifestyle of the individual, but will probably include greater confidence and awareness.

CONFIDENCE

A healthy body is bound to promote a healthy and more enterprising mind. This fitness, acquired through judo training, plus the pleasures of progress, all contribute to the development of a quality many people lack — confidence. Martial artists are usually among the most positive people, and they exude confidence in most situations.

It should be appreciated, though, that over-confidence can be a dangerous quality to possess. A simple example of such a danger can be observed in *judoka* who believe they are more capable than they actually are; this usually results in the over-confident practitioner being thrown around the *dojo* by an under-estimated partner.

However, providing that progress and confidence are supported by a stable, analytical attitude, then the lucky possessor of this new-found quality will be successful in most walks of life. The following simple rule of thumb, which was introduced many years ago by Sun Tse, a Chinese warrior of repute, should be committed to memory by all *judoka*:

Know the enemy and know yourself, in a hundred battles you will never be in peril. When you are ignorant of the enemy but know yourself, your chances of winning and losing are equal.

If ignorant of both your enemy and yourself, you are certain in every battle to be in peril.

The eyes do not miss even the slightest change and the ears listen well in all directions.

This rather philosophical statement is simply stressing the dangers of over-confidence and lack of awareness. It should also be understood that the reference to 'battles' does not necessarily mean warlike combat, but could also apply to social or business situations.

ZANSHIN AWARENESS

There are many examples of martial arts masters apparently possessing a magical ability to read minds or see into the future. One student described an example of such an incident which occurred during the late 19th century outside a Japanese judo *dojo*.

My lesson was concluded and Sensei left the *dojo* and walked to the edge of the river, where he lay down and fell asleep.

I decided to test the *zanshin* of my Sensei — after all, he had continually been stressing awareness throughout the previous lesson, and here he was, completely unguarded and asleep.

I crept to the river's edge and raised the wooden practice sword, normally used for self defence tuition. I intended to tap my Master on the head and utter a 'kia' (war-like scream) to warn him of his vulnerability.

I raised the sword and was about to strike when, suddenly, I felt a blow to my stomach. Sensei then executed a flying stomach throw, dumping me in the river. I stumbled ashore, to grasp his extended hand — he appeared to be offering assistance back onto dry land . . . without warning, he twisted my arm in an armlock, I found myself trapped, face down.

A few moments later I was freed. Sensei stared into my eyes and said: 'Over confident, no *zanshin* and incorrect stance.'

I was amazed . . . how had my Master known of my intentions?

This story is one of many well known to martial artists. It demonstrates what is possible when one reaches the advanced level of fitness. There is no magic involved, simply *zanshin* — awareness. This Zen-like capability is only perfected after protracted study. Breathing exercises (see pages 67-68) and meditation (see page 66) are helpful in developing *zanshin*. Once acquired, the judo student becomes aware of having generally more tolerance, adaptability and mental flexibility than non-martial artists.

Once again, it should be noted that awareness plays a role outside the *dojo* too. By being aware the individual looks and sees, listens and hears; they are also able to anticipate occurrences in almost every situation. Awareness improves general performance in all areas of life, a prime example, of course, is Japanese success in commerce and industry.

EVERYDAY LIFE

Modern society is the greatest creator of stress and fear. And judo practitioners regularly deal with different forms of stress and fear — every lesson creates these invisible demons that infiltrate the combatant's demeanour. Individuals who allow such distractions to permeate their thoughts will almost certainly be thrown or armlocked by their partner.

These invisible demons present themselves in various forms. The most common in the judo *dojo* is the club member who is seen regularly throwing higher grades. Invariably, insecure *judoka*, some of a higher grade, avoid such members because of the fear of being thrown and 'losing face'. Outside of the *dojo*, these demons strike day after day, again in various forms. A good example of such stress is the arrival in the morning post of letters from the tax office or other such authorities. The addressee immediately experiences a surge of panic, which is created by the reputation such government departments have developed over the years.

An experienced martial artist regularly practising their chosen Way should never be upset by the notorious club member or the official communication. By being constantly alert to penalties that are paid for lack of *zanshin* (awareness), the *judoka* gradually develops the ability to deal with not only fear and stress but even, if necessary, with death. Armed with this attitude and awareness, the martial artist will more easily deal with the problems created by modern-day society.

Business

To conduct any sort of business transaction with a true martial artist, especially from the judo fraternity, is an experience never to be forgotten. Such individuals are not only articulate almost to the point of exasperation, but the concise planning ability of these 20th-century strategists has frustrated many a business opponent. Their dedication to all matters is impressive. They are undisputed masters of the boardroom.

Remember the Japanese success in industry, all achieved by the *samurai*-like approach to business — this in itself should encourage judo students to persevere with their training. With regular practice, accompanied by academic study, the experienced *judoka* will eventually realize that their powers of concentration and their ability to direct effort towards specific projects has improved. At work, complicated assignments will represent *randori* (free practice) and the practitioner will gradually improve their all-round professional performance. Physical and mental fitness will be obvious, the result being a transformation into a respected, confident member of society.

Friendship

Established traditional practitioners enjoy membership of an élite worldwide club, sharing an *ésprit de corps* similar to that of ancient *samurai* warriors. Friendships conceived in judo are for life, and it is interesting to observe that student–instructor relationships sometimes continue for many years, even after the student reaches an advanced level of ability.

There is no stronger bond anywhere in the world than that of true martial artists — *judoka, karateka, aikidoka, kendoka.* All share similar disappointments and successes whilst travelling their *budo* journey. To share membership of this fraternity, as well as being a valuable contributor to social order, are the ultimate benefits to be gained from judo training.

Improved health

After 20 visits to hospital and being close to death, a 10-year-old boy decided to join a judo club. After two years regular training his condition improved so much it was possible to include karate in his martial arts training. At 13 years he achieved promotion to high grades in judo and karate. Despite the fact he still suffers from asthma, the condition has improved so that hospital visits are less frequent. The high standard of fitness he has acquired and the breathing exercises (see pages 67-68) involved in training have aided the regression of this unpleasant ailment.

A second example, that of a car accident victim, gives an impressive indication of what dedicated martial arts training can achieve. Having experienced nine months of hospitalization, the victim of a serious motor accident resorted to drink and drugs to deal with the extreme pain created by the numerous operations necessary to rebuild his body. After being discharged from hospital this seriously damaged individual, was held together with steel bars in the joints of his arms and legs. Psychologically, he found it very difficult to come to terms with the traumatic experience of the accident and he also became grossly overweight, his overall condition aggravated by the drink and drugs.

For some unknown reason this unfortunate person was attracted to judo. After two years' painful study the success achieved between instructor and student was nothing short of a miracle. No longer was this accident victim a physically incapable, psychological wreck, but a healthy, likeable human being whose body was capable of functioning normally and who had regained a more positive approach to life. Instructor and student remain friends to this day.

Another martial arts 'miracle' is the case of a Japanese *budo* master, buried for hours in an avalanche. Examinations by doctors resulted in their worst fears; it was formally announced that this master would never be able to practise martial arts again, and it was touch and go whether he would even live.

The magic of *budo*, however, disagreed with this diagnosis, and within weeks the world-famous Sensei Nakayama was leading students in strenuous *dojo* training sessions. Subsequent examinations by doctors, amazed at his recovery, eventually affirmed that Sensei Nakayama's years of dedicated *budo* training greatly contributed to his speedy recuperation.

Such examples as these are the tip of the iceberg. Instructors all over the world have interesting stories to tell, such as men, women and children experiencing relief from arthritis, victims of stress enjoying better all-round health, improvements in blood circulation, and regression of numerous minor (and some major) conditions. There is nothing really magical about such occurrences. Most are attained by individuals who eventually reach a stage in training where mind and body function as one unit. Spiritual healers seek this condition in their patients, so it is a reasonable comparison to suggest that all martial arts are a form of physical spiritual healing.

MIND — BODY — SPIRIT

The ultimate goal of all *judoka* should be a healthy body, mind and spirit, functioning as one unit. On the occasions when there is little or no enthusiasm for practice, the student must somehow summon up the energy and self discipline to visit the *dojo*. Regular training is not only essential for physical fitness, but also for the development of the mind and spirit. Regular practice also enables the student to programme their mind and body to such a fine pitch that techniques are performed without conscious thought. But this spontaneous execution of all judo techniques can only be achieved by a committed and wholehearted application of traditional doctrines.

4
JUDO TECHNIQUES AND TRADITIONAL METHODS OF PRACTICE

This chapter is not intended to be a comprehensive technical examination of all judo techniques and methods of practice. Readers wanting to explore overall aspects of the art should consult a qualified instructor, or alternatively obtain a suitable technical publication.

The actual combat techniques of judo are divided into five sections, as follows:

- *Tachiwaza*, throwing
- *Osae-waza*, holding
- *Kansetsu-waza*, armlocking
- *Shime-waza*, strangling
- *Atemi-waza*, striking vital points

However, before we look at these we need to consider two important preliminaries, the warming-up period in a class and *ukemi*, the art of breakfalling.

WARMING UP

An integral part of any physical activity, be it a martial art or sport, is a period of warming-up exercises. Judo, being an extremely strenuous pursuit, relies on special stretching and limbering-up exercises called calisthenics.

Most instructors adopt their own particular system of warming up, so it is not uncommon for students to experience slightly different approaches to this part of the lesson. Approximately 15-20 minutes is sufficient time to prepare the body for strenuous activity.

Limbering-up exercises, especially stretching, are very important prior to a lesson.

UKEMI, THE ART OF FALLING

The importance of *ukemi* cannot be over-stressed. Anyone involved in the practice of judo who is unable to perform safe breakfalls to the left and right, as well as backwards, is a dangerous liability.

Unfortunately certain sports *judoka* are guilty of neglecting the ability to fall correctly, because of the possibility of maximum points being awarded against them in a contest if they do fall. Consequently, whilst engaged in ordinary club practice, their continuing bad habits invariably result in serious accidents. This is unwise, bordering on the dangerous, and clubs tending to neglect *ukemi* should be avoided.

Traditional teachers are very strict when it comes to breakfall training, and it is not unusual for beginners to spend weeks mastering the art before engaging in actual throws. Most instructors devise their own system of teaching students how to fall, but as long as the end result is a safe *judoka* performing satisfactory *ukemi*, it does not really matter how the instructor approaches this aspect of training. Usually, *ukemi* practice follows the warming-up exercises, and is performed by the whole class including the high grades.

Ukemi (breakfalling techniques) should always be carried out under the supervision of a qualified instructor.

The period of time needed to perfect breakfalls differs with each student, but a *bona fide* traditional instructor will not allow anyone to engage in throwing practice until they have mastered the art of falling.

TACHIWAZA, THROWING

The traditional method of throwing is probably the most misunderstood aspect of judo. The traditional system of throwing is based on *kuzushi* (breaking of balance), accompanied by *tai-sabaki* (the use of the feet). These skills are well known to the traditional teacher and will be explained to the beginner during the early stages of training.

A very frustrating sight is of some sports *judoka*, who obviously has no understanding of the methods of *kuzushi* or *tai-sabaki* but who is blessed with upper-body strength,

Koshi-guruma (loin wheel) — a variation on a hip throw.

Tomoe-nage (stomach throw) — a very advanced technique.

dragging or dumping their partners to the ground using sheer brute force only. This type of judo is deplorable, and practitioners of this style invariably cause regular injuries to partners, and become very unpopular with their colleagues. Fortunately they don't usually last very long practising such untraditional styles of judo, and invariably retire during their early years. Alternatively, they hang around the club, engaging in *kuchi-waza* (talking technique).

The correct execution of *kuzushi* (breaking of balance) can have devastating effects.

Kuzushi, **breaking balance**

There are numerous throws in the Kano-*Kodokan* syllabus, all relying on the breaking of balance before execution of a fall. *Kuzushi* can be achieved by anyone, especially people of smaller stature. Very little physical strength is required, and throws activated with *kuzushi* are without doubt the most powerful.

A student examining the art of creating instability should study it with the attitude of a scientist. There are dozens of ways to unbalance an opponent in eight main directions, and success depends primarily on the ability to understand the principle of *ju* — gentleness, as discussed in the previous chapter.

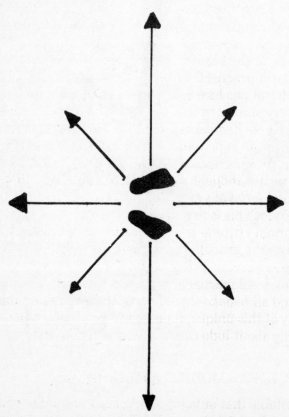

Kuzushi (breaking of balance) — there are eight primary directions.

Kata, form

Normally, instructors will devote lengthy periods to the practice of certain basic throws, allowing the practitioner to build up a repertoire of throws over a number of months. One method of practising throws for advanced students is by utilizing the system of *kata* training. Descriptions of the word *kata* have varied over the years, but in simple terms this useful method of practice can be explained as follows.

In an attempt to develop their fighting system, the *samurai* warriors of old designed patterns of particular throwing techniques that were tried and tested in actual combat. These patterns, or forms as they were sometimes called, were practised repeatedly until the combatant was able to perform them at will. Eventually these forms were passed on from master to student, in effect becoming the 'notebooks' of the *samurai.* Patterns, now referred to as *kata,* are still practised by 20th-century *judoka*; although certain alterations have been made, essentially they remain very similar to the forms created many years ago.

In the Kano-*Kodokan* system there are eight primary *katas* which the *budo* traditionalist can study. Many advanced *judoka* create their own personal *katas* of self defence, as it is thought by certain non-Japanese that the old Oriental *katas* of years gone by have no place in modern judo. This is not the case, though.

The formal attitude adopted during *kata* training not only assists the practitioner to develop his art, but also is an extremely useful system of developing *zanshin* (awareness). All martial arts possess their own traditional forms, and all *budoka* should devote considerable time to the study of this unique approach to development as everything about judo can be found in judo *katas.*

OSAE-WAZA, IMMOBILIZATION HOLDS

It is inevitable that antagonists engaged in combat will find themselves fighting on the ground. The art of *osae-waza* provides the judo adept with a number of suitable

Kesa-gatame (scarf hold)

Tate-shihogatame (upper four quarters or straddle hold)

Osae-waza (the art of holding).

ways of immobilizing an opponent on their back.

The object of holding one's partner on their back is to immobilize them for 30 seconds, or until such time as a submission by tapping is offered. When this occurs, an advantage is declared to the holder.

This aspect of judo is energetic, as well as interesting, and can be enjoyed by all students during the early days of training. As long as the various safety rules are adhered to, practitioners can enjoy extended periods of groundwork exercise.

KANSETSU-WAZA, ARMLOCKING

Locking a partner's arm joints is an extension of groundwork. However, skilful exponents of armlocks invariably utilize their skills in the standing position. It is

Ude-gatame (forearm lock)

Juji-gatame (cross armlock)

Kansetsu-waza (arm locking techniques) should only be practised under the supervision of a qualified instructor.

an extremely useful method of self defence, and anyone interested in self defence normally specializes in *kansetsu-waza*.

Armlocking techniques require total control by the applicator. An angry or violent disposition will almost certainly result in serious damage to a partner's arm. To apply an effective armlock also requires great skill, as well

Waki-gatame (armpit lock)

Ude-garami (entangled or figure-of-eight armlock)

as an understanding of the scientific aspects involved in a lock being used. Strength is not required; indeed, practitioners must realize from the outset that locking a partner's limb is dangerous and can, if not controlled, result in a dislocation or break. The rules of safety therefore dictate that, once a lock is applied correctly, the recipient must not be injured. As soon as the effect of the armlock is felt, submission should be indicated by tapping the applicant firmly two or three times.

There are in fact many armlocks, with variations peculiar to particular instructors, and *judoka* skilled in the art of *kansetsu-waza* are usually of the black belt rank. They are capable of applying an effective armlock within seconds, thus rendering an opponent helpless or seriously injured. It has often been said that armlocking techniques are an art within an art.

SHIME-WAZA, STRANGULATION

Japanese masters have developed this lethal aspect of judo into a speedy method of controlling an opponent. Within seconds the recipient of a strangle can be rendered unconscious (or even dead!). Generally, *shime-waza* techniques are utilized during groundwork. However, many skilled exponents are able to use certain modified strangles in a standing position. Once again, safety rules apply.

To practise these techniques is relatively easy. The applicant simply applies a particular strangulation on a passive partner, who submits by tapping immediately a positive effect is experienced. Again, strength is not required, and small people tend to be very adept in the art of *shime-waza.*

In free practice or contests, it is not uncommon to witness victims of strangulation techniques lying unconscious on the mat. In certain Oriental *dojos* submission is sometimes not considered, and practitioners simply strangle each other out at will. This is not recommended.

Many Western judo exponents tend to underestimate the effectiveness of *shime-waza*, the result being that a number of potentially dangerous situations have developed in past competitions. During one major tournament a well-known player nearly strangled his opponent to death. It would be fair to say that during the hectic fight for supremacy the insatiable desire to win encouraged this particular sports *judoka* to throw caution and ethics to the wind, the result being near tragedy.

Nami-juji-jime (normal cross strangle)

Hadaka-jime (naked strangle)

Shime-waza (the art of strangulation) — such techniques should only be practised under the supervision of a qualified instructor.

For these reasons it is my opinion that not only strangulation but also armlock techniques should not be taught to or practised by children below the age of 16.

ATEMI-WAZA, STRIKING TECHNIQUES

Included in the Kano-*Kodokan* syllabus is the ancient art of *atemi-waza*. Not often practised by Western *judoka*, this system includes blocking, punching and kicking to vital areas of the body.

It is not possible to practise this highly advanced form of combat on a partner. Usually special equipment is utilized such as a punch-bag or *makiwara* (striking board). It is a lethal aspect of *budo* training and should not be misused.

RANDORI, FREE PRACTICE

An important facet of all martial arts training is the time devoted to some kind of sparring-type activity. This is the occasion practitioners are able to test their fighting techniques, as well as attitude, discipline and control.

Depending on their standard of *ukemi* (breakfalling), students are introduced to *randori* at various stages of their training. This new and exciting world of judo affords practitioners the opportunity to test themselves in actual combat, albeit in a controlled environment. It is an essential aspect of training, and all *judoka* can progress physically, as well as spiritually, through *randori.*

Because of the combative element in free practice, it is necessary that both antagonists adopt an appropriate code of conduct throughout the session. Politeness and respect should be injected into the proceedings, as well as a *samurai*-like approach to actual techniques of survival. There is no place in traditional *randori* for cheating or dirty tricks. The occasion should in fact be an exhausting but enjoyable experience shared by two ethical participants struggling to perfect the development of their respective characters. This is achieved through their combined attempt to perform skilful judo techniques; depending on what agreement exists beforehand, armlocks or strangles may well be included.

Certain exponents often treat a *randori* session as a representation of life. They accept the risk of being thrown as synonymous with the stress of dealing with the trials and tribulations of modern society.

The benefits of this type of training are many. Not only

can participants progress in actual style and technique, but they are able to identify their various weaknesses, as well as psychological inadequacies. Individuals who fail to take advantage of the occasion to pinpoint such defects are not engaging the true judo Way. It is often said that a person's conduct on the mat is identical to their attitude outside the *dojo*, and in my experience this is true. It is not often that an individual is able to confront safely the demons of fear and trepidation. *Randori*, however, is such an occasion. Throughout a session of free practice the judo student is constantly face to face with the fear of being thrown to the mat. His control of emotional feelings on these occasions will contribute to his overall development.

Having reached a stage in progress where *randori* can be practised with a reasonable degree of proficiency, students suddenly have access to a whole new and exciting world of judo. The age-old natural urge to compete with others in a physical fashion can be exhausted. With correct application of the principles of *Kodokan* judo, students should have little or no difficulty in enjoying a lifetime of martial arts study.

5
PRACTICE OUTSIDE THE CLUB

Because of the nature of judo, it is impossible to engage in any form of home practice. However, there are certain exercises that can be conducted at home that will greatly improve flexibility of the individual for whatever style is practised.

All of the warming-up exercises performed in the *dojo* can be performed at home. Not only will such activity improve the practitioner's judo, but a general feeling of well-being will result.

JOGGING OR WALKING

The heart, being a muscle, requires as much attention as the rest of the body. Aerobic exercises such as walking or jogging are a good way of developing the heart muscle so that it can cope with the rigours of judo training. Sport or traditional *judoka* should regularly treat themselves to a jogging/walking session of approximately 3 miles, while advanced practitioners frequently engage in extensive jogging, the result being that their stamina during *randori* (free practice) or competition is greatly improved. This is an ideal method of maintaining fitness that can be utilized when away from the *dojo*.

YOGA

An effective method of improving general circulation, fitness and suppleness is to undertake simple yoga exercises and positions. These can be learned from books — there are many available — but it is advisable to attend a class to learn how to do things properly. If it is a good class you will also be shown breathing exercises and forms of meditation (see below).

A yoga session of 30 minutes, once or twice a day, will greatly improve the individual's condition. Men, who tend to be less supple than women, will find it of particular value.

MEDITATION

The art of meditation is a complicated subject in its own right, and there are many excellent publications available to introduce the *judoka* to this method of spiritual development. Meditation ably assists both traditional and sport judo; the physical activity of a free practice (*randori*) or contest is in effect an act of 'moving meditation', with participants deeply attempting to see the way to success and development.

By regular meditation, the *judoka* is able to improve concentration, to such an extent that a clear, comprehensive picture is formed in the mind during judo practice. This is essential to attain spiritual development.

RELAXATION

Eventually, the judo student will realize that their concentrated, diligent study has developed the ability to 'switch-off' outside thoughts, such as domestic or professional problems. The absence of these ever-present demons are moments of great peace and relaxation. This state can only be achieved by individuals prepared to commit all energies — physical, mental and spiritual — to their training.

BREATHING

An often neglected, yet important, aspect of training and of life generally is the *samurai* art of breathing. During the practice of martial arts, breathing is an integral part of every technique. It is important for the practitioner to breath in and out with a rhythm which is suited to their own body performance. Ideally, the inhalation should occur when commencing a throw and the exhalation completed with the throw.

It should be appreciated that the human body requires a regular supply of oxygen in order to function efficiently and that oxygen is essential for clarity of mind. The air we breathe contains oxygen. However, the air found in hot climates or buildings is often of poor quality and does not provide an adequate source for the oxygen-hungry athlete. *Judoka* should understand that a poor supply of oxygen results in a rapid deterioration of mental and physical ability. It is therefore suggested that, during meditation practice, the art of breathing be performed, as follows:

- Adopt a relaxed sitting or standing posture.
- Exhale slowly and deeply through the mouth, pulling the stomach in, until the lungs are empty.
- At the point of emptiness, slowly, and with control, breathe in through the nose, attempting to achieve total inhalation after 20 seconds.
- Hold the breath for a maximum of 10 seconds, then exhale, with control, through the mouth, achieving full exhalation after 20 seconds.
- Repeat several times.

Prior to a *randori* session or competition, deep breathing of this nature will create a pleasant, calming effect within the individual, culminating in the ability to deal in a positive, progressive way with the opponent. Traditional or sports *judoka* can benefit greatly from deep breathing.

When experiencing any kind of stress, this breathing exercise carried out in fresh air quickly calms you and encourages great clarity of mind. This exercise is a must for all martial artists, regardless of style.

DIET

One of the greatest problems facing Western society today is 'What to eat'. There has been much publicity of late, highlighting certain foods as being riddled with harmful bacteria and additives which are dangerous to the consumer. *Judoka* cannot really disagree, on the subject of diet that 'We are what we eat' is a fact of life.

Whatever style of judo is practised, the body requires regular sustenance in the form of water, protein, carbohydrate, fibre and fat, plus vitamins and other trace nutrients. Despite an individual's preference for various foods, there are certain very important items that must be eaten by active sportspeople and martial artists.

Protein
Protein is vital for building and repairing of muscle tissue and can be found in the following foods: eggs, fish, meat, soya beans, milk, nuts, rice and corn. For practitioners who are vegetarian, some form of protein replacement must be adopted, and tofu is an excellent and nutritional alternative to meat.

Carbohydrates
Again, this is a vital food which provides energy and must be taken on board at regular intervals, especially before a long, hard period of activity. Carbohydrates can be found in bread, pasta, potatoes, cereals, and rice. An example of the importance of carbohydrate can be found in the famous pasta parties the night before a marathon event.

Fibre
This element of the diet is frequently overlooked, resulting in an occasional break-down of the digestive system. A valuable function of fibre is the absorption of bile acids, which are necessary for digestion but can ultimately have

a bad effect upon the health of the intestine. Vegetables, fruit, nuts, wholegrains and pulses are good sources of fibre.

Fat

Generally, too much fat is consumed in the West, especially saturated animal fats which can cause heart disease. It is important to cut down on fat and use polyunsaturated fat as found in many margarines, or monounsaturated fat found in olive oil.

Strenuous training must be accompanied by a balanced, sensible diet. It should be remembered that for every hour's physical activity, energy is used at the rate of approximately 1,000 calories per hour, depending on the weight of the *judoka* and the amount of effort injected into the session. It is the responsibility of all *judoka* to understand their own particular requirements. A poor diet can have a debilitating effect on the energetic practitioner, leading to serious illness if not rectified.

Dedicated study of any martial art will lead to an intimate understanding of the body's requirements.

6
TRADITION v. SPORT

Despite many years' study, often resulting in numerous competition successes, certain practitioners never manage to identify the many differences that exist between traditional and sport judo. This ignorance is not the fault of the individuals, but stems from the overwhelming influence of the sport and non-traditional instructors who regularly advertise judo as simply an Olympic fighting activity. It is not uncommon for a non-Japanese practitioner, when asked the meaning of the Japanese word *judo*, to reply with statements so detached from the true translation and meaning as to defy publication.

In 1983 a famous European competitor was asked to give an opinion on *kata* training. 'I have no time for *kata*, I'm only interested in winning. If I don't keep the medals coming in, I'll be dropped from the team.' This statement aptly illuminates the pressure on and stress experienced by an international player.

COMPETITION JUDO

To the spectator, a judo contest can be most unentertaining — two frantic players pulling each other around the mat, relying primarily on brute strength to gain an advantage. It is not uncommon to witness a player winning a gold medal by grabbing a leg and simply dumping an opponent on the mat in a most un-judo-like fashion, the execution of such a technique usually results in a minimum score of three or five points. Such a style of judo is completely contrary to the Kano-*Kodokan* way, and does not contribute to the development of one's character.

Traditionalists all over the world frequently argue that this style of judo is destroying the historical background and philosophy of the art. To an extent, this might well be true. However the players themselves cannot be held as the sole cause of this situation. There are other circumstances contributing to a general decline of the gentle Way.

Rules and regulations

There are a number of operational rules applicable to contests. In the main, they apply to scoring points, as well as safety and weight categories. A contest is supervised by one referee, plus corner judges, although these officials sometimes disagree on decisions. This situation has been known to result in unpleasant scenes involving coaches, or even spectators.

Financial aid

A tremendous amount of money is invested by governments and sports councils in supporting their national judo squads. This money is invariably paid to the association or federation controlling the selection of the teams. Consequently, great operational and political pressure is experienced by the coaches who are faced with the task of producing winning teams. In such conditions standards, as viewed in the traditional sense, are bound to deteriorate.

Personal stress

On the day of an important contest, the urge for personal success, accompanied by additional political stress, creates a competitor who invariably resorts to desperate or unorthodox methods of achieving victory. This is not only contrary to the spirit of *budo*, but can also be very dangerous for competitors. It is not uncommon for sports players to experience the occasional broken or dislocated limb — this is par for the course. However, the trauma of modern-day tournaments has created more serious accidents, leading to amputated legs and broken necks. These tragic situations could well have been avoided were it not for the frantic requirement to win at all costs.

Differences in training

Sport and traditional methods of training differ. Whereas the athlete tends to concentrate on the development of strength, stamina and skill (in that order), the pure traditionalist has a different set of priorities, i.e. skill, stamina, followed by (theoretically) no strength! This creates a situation where, in a tournament, the skilled traditionalist might well be scientifically an expert in the art but, because of lack of contest experience, accompanied by an unfamiliarity with the inhibiting rules applying to competitions, a sports *judoka* might be the victor.

On the other hand, if a pure *judoka* were to find himself involved in actual real-life combat with a sports judo athlete, it is more likely that the traditionalist, having trained for life or death situations, would have the advantage over the sportsman.

In certain cases, purists extend their martial arts to include, perhaps, karate or *aikido* training. It is not widely known, but the three arts — judo, *shotokan* karate and *aikido* — do in fact function extremely well as one complete system of *budo*, and there are a number of practising black belts studying judo and *shotokan* karate.

Retirement

Most sports judo players retire around the age of 30, although there have been certain successful athletes who have progressed into their 30s. After retirement it is possible for worthy fighters to acquire coaching positions within their parent organization, although, in the main, players of area or occasional national standard fade into obscurity, relegated to the precincts of their home club.

The traditional *judoka* never retires. Having achieved maximum physical fitness, the dedicated practitioner should continue to study and practise until the day they die. Judo is for life.

SPORTING BENEFITS

All sport creates fitness, as well as a code of discipline adopted by competitors. In team events *ésprit de corps* is created, the result being that individuals develop the ability to contribute to a team effort. Stamina, strength, as well as devotion to training are all associated with sport judo. Despite traditional criticism, these benefits should not be overlooked.

Top judo players have access to first class facilities, including leisure centres, running tracks, special weight-training programmes. Experienced coaches devote their expertise to the education of these athletes, and at the end of the day any practitioner who qualifies for a place in a national judo team is to be congratulated for this achievement alone. The standards of fitness are extremely high, especially at international level.

SUCCESSFUL COMPETITORS

In spite of the many questionable facets of sport judo, it must be said that not all competitors are unorthodox barbarians waging destruction on their colleagues. On the contrary, there are certain practitioners who are skilled, ethical *judoka* who have achieved phenomenal success for their respective countries.

These players are renowned for regularly executing the ultimate judo technique — a perfect throw, achieving maximum points. To observe such expert athletes at work is an experience never to be forgotten. The spectacle of one of these 20th-century warriors executing such a technique under inhibiting tournament conditions is a truly exciting experience. Spectators usually erupt into an explosion of applause lasting for several minutes, and on these occasions even traditionalists have to admit that this is a martial art being performed to near perfection.

It would be unfair to list examples of these sporting personalities for fear of inadvertently omitting someone. Suffice to say they hail from various countries, including Japan, France, Britain, Germany, Belgium Korea and Holland. Many of these judo 'legends' have retired from active competition; others still represent their country. But it is interesting to note that in the majority of cases the initial basic training acquired by the player was in the traditional way.

The present-day method of training champions in Japan is to detect potential *judoka* while they are still at school. Instructors then move heaven and earth to navigate such potentials into university *dojos*, with one object in mind — to produce a champion. According to Master Mochizuki, 'All they think about is making a grand champion, so that schools and universities can bask in the reflected glory.'

Despite this departure from the traditional Kano-*Kodokan* way, one Japanese world sporting champion emerged as the greatest *judoka* of all time — Yasuhiro Yamashita. Yamashita's traditional grounding in judo resulted in repeated successes, and on his retirement he remained unbeaten world and Olympic champion. While still a young man, Yamashita retired from competition to dedicate himself to teaching in direct line with Dr Kano's way.

The style of Yamashita can be described as judo in its purest form. All successes were achieved with clean, safe techniques, resulting in maximum points. When questioned about his judo career, he made the following statement.

Competition was only a moment in my life, the competition period does not last forever, while teaching judo occupies a whole lifetime! Being a champion wasn't a goal for me, it was a stroke of luck!

MAKING A DECISION

Before embarking on any judo training programme, the potential student should pose the question 'Do I practise sport judo or do I study traditional judo?'

Only personal experience over a number of years reveals the various advantages (and disadvantages) of both styles. It would therefore be sensible to commence in the traditional style and include sporting judo in the general framework of one's study at a later date. This system appears to have been very successful for many champions of the day who, having concluded a period of competition judo, simply revert to their original traditional study without any difficulty. Such a plan seems to be a very practical way of dealing with the problem. Of course, personalities and requirements do differ, and there are bound to be certain people who have no interest in traditional Japanese martial arts but who lean towards direct entry to the sport versions, where they can achieve many benefits.

7
JUDO AS SELF DEFENCE

Everyone has a right to feel safe in their own home or on the streets. However, conditions in modern society are such that, in certain countries, personal safety for residents is becoming a very serious problem. Despite the almost unmanageable situations created by regular occurrences of violence, robbery, murder and rape, police authorities are responding by doing everything possible to reduce the risks.

But crimes of violence do occur — every day of the week, 52 weeks a year — and, in spite of police proficiency, the victim is the one who has to deal with the situation. There is often no time to summon assistance, and unless some sort of immediate evasive action is taken, the innocent person will end up injured, raped or even dead.

A person under attack has every right to defend themselves. In some countries, firearms are permitted and it is not uncommon for a private citizen to shoot an attacker in self defence. However, in countries such as Britain the carrying of firearms is not permitted, and legislation is such that a victim, using more than the minimum amount of force necessary to defend themselves, could end up in court. Furthermore, in certain countries like Britain, the law does not allow the possession of anything which can be described as an offensive weapon, including specially-adapted items such as a sharpened comb or a knife. Such rules apply particularly to martial artists; any judo practitioner who over-reacts in a confrontation, using unnecessary violence against an attacker, will more than likely find themselves charged with serious criminal offences.

A second *dan* black belt of a European Judo Association was returning home from a party. At approximately 11 pm this experienced practitioner was approached by three unarmed youths who stopped him and demanded money. The black belt immediately responded by grabbing the obvious leader and striking him on the side of the neck with a lethal *atemi-waza* technique. Turning to the remaining two youths, he seized one and viciously applied an armlock, resulting in a broken elbow joint. By this time, the final member of the trio was running away, only to be chased by the intended victim, who savagely threw him to the ground, breaking three ribs.

Back at the scene of the incident, local residents had gathered to assist the leader of the gang, who was semiconscious and foaming at the mouth. Being an epileptic, the blow to a vital spot on the neck had apparently activated a fit.

The three would-be assailants were admitted to hospital in a serious condition. It was later discovered they were nothing more than young teenagers. Parents of the injured prepared charges against the black belt who, it transpired, was an experienced instructor, highly skilled in the traditional ways of judo. He was eventually charged with three offences of grievous bodily harm and sentenced to six months' imprisonment.

This sentence might seem a little harsh. However, the prosecution revealed that the judo black belt was an expert in *ju-jitsu* and that he had made a study of self defence against multiple assailants. It was therefore submitted to the judge and jury that such an adept should have been capable of neutralizing the assailants without causing injury. This unfortunate incident in which an experienced *judoka* acted in anger clearly demonstrates the importance of self-control. In my opinion, his behaviour was a sign of spiritual immaturity.

WHAT IS SELF DEFENCE?

There is no official definition of self defence, but generally speaking any evasive or physical act that results in the protection of persons or property can be considered self defence, and this includes avoiding potential confrontations. A high degree of personal security can only be achieved with the application of day-to-day commonsense.

Let us return for a moment to the over-violent black belt. Had he decided to *avoid* the confrontation by walking away, then that would have been an example of commonsense. Better still, a highly-trained martial artist should not have been out on the streets late at night. In today's social environment, such conduct is nothing more than an advertisement for trouble.

Unfortunately, though, any human being, regardless of age or lifestyle, may be attacked. Statistics suggest women and young girls are more vulnerable than men — the reason for this is obvious. But there are numerous commonsense preparations and precautions that individuals can adopt to their lifestyle, the object being to avoid confrontation. The following recommendations apply to men, women and young girls:

- Avoid quiet, deserted locations, especially woods, parks, etc.
- Avoid groups standing on street corners, hovering around cars, etc.
- Females and young girls should, where possible, travel with a friend or relative, and carefully plan every journey they intend to make.
- Avoid sitting in empty carriages on trains without corridors.
- Avoid, where possible, speaking to strangers, especially when approached for any form of help. This rule especially applies to women and young girls.
- Do not hitch-hike or accept lifts with strangers, even if the vehicle is occupied by a female.

- If travelling at night, stick to well-lit busy routes.
- Ensure that a security chain is attached to the front and back door of domestic premises.
- Always attempt to identify callers before opening the door.
- Unidentified callers presenting themselves as officials should be challenged and asked for an identity card.
- Avoid dark multistorey car parks. This rule especially applies to females — where possible they should park their cars in the street or in a busy open car park.
- Parents should exercise strict control of the activities of their children. Under no circumstances should youngsters be allowed to lead uncontrolled social lives.

The above precautions are just a few commonsense considerations that will help you avoid getting attacked. Obviously it is impossible to discuss every set of circumstances, but avoidance rather than confrontation should be the motto of every practising *judoka*. It should only be necessary to engage in actual physical self defence if there is no other method of resolving the predicament.

WHAT TO DO IF YOU ARE ATTACKED

For the *judoka* who has mastered the art of permanent awareness, *zanshin*, in theory any situation requiring self defence should be visible well in advance. The experienced adept should never be caught offguard. The attitude outside the *dojo* should be total awareness at all times, allowing you to avoid any situation that could possibly lead to violence.

Attitude
At the first sign of attack, assuming there is time, positive controlling action should be adopted, accompanied by a suitable emotional and spiritual approach to the situation.

A *judoka* faced with an attacker should immediately consider the size, stance and general deportment of the

Basic hip throw

Armlock being used in self defence

Self defence techniques.

adversary. This analysis must be completed instantly, because the answers to these questions will affect whatever self defence technique is to be utilized. For example, if a protagonist is 197 cm (6 feet 6 inches) and the defender 160 cm (5 feet 3 inches), it is highly unlikely that any throw in which the defender's arms go around the neck of the attacker will be used.

The defender must be able to apply all thought to the job of self preservation. There should be no mental activity directed to uncertainty or fear, and any physical move must be carried out in such a way that the attacker is immobilized immediately. Certain *judoka* have favourite techniques, i.e. armlocks, foot-sweeps, or strangulation applications, but in a real fight, depending on their degree of skill, the effectiveness of such methods might be minimal.

Thinking time

A victim threatened with attack or held hostage is said to have 'thinking time', which should be used to analyse fully the situation and choose a suitable method of defence. This could include some sort of verbal negotiation or trick designed to persuade the attacker to abandon their intentions. The ability to speak clearly, with confidence is vital in self defence. Martial artists, with their razor-sharp, analytical minds should have less difficulty in negotiating for their lives than people with no martial arts training.

The chances of survival using judo are good, providing the practitioner remains calm and chooses a technique to suit the occasion. An apprentice with only a few months training will stand less chance of success than an experienced black belt. It is therefore up to the individual to be fully aware of their own capabilities.

Sporting martial artists are generally physically very strong and fast, but have a limited knowledge of their particular discipline. Dedicated training for the contest arena has usually developed favourite techniques that may be useful for winning tournaments but might not be suitable for life or death combat. It therefore stands to reason that a sports person will stand a little less chance of survival. However, general fitness, etc., will be an invaluable asset.

The traditionalist, on the other hand, will have examined and developed all available judo techniques. In some cases, they may well have the experience of *ju-jitsu* and, because of their *samurai*-like approach to training, they will be able to function very successfully in an actual fight. Their skill at armlocking and 'instant throwing' will prove a big surprise for the attacker. The general habit of the experienced traditionalist is always to remain alert — this will be an invaluable contribution to survival.

Initial response

In the absence of any thinking time the defender must respond with a suitable technique that will neutralize the situation. Suitable judo self defence methods are armlocks, hold-downs and throws, as well as strikes to vital areas of the body. The use of strangle holds should only be adopted by experienced practitioners, though, for obvious reasons — it could be quite easy to strangle someone to death during a frantic struggle.

THE ULTIMATE METHOD OF DEFENCE

There have been numerous attempts to create the ultimate method of self defence. It is my belief that no such art exists, but it goes without saying that some martial arts will serve as better systems of defence than others.

It is interesting to note that certain martial artists have dedicated their lives to training in both judo and *Shotokan* karate. It is not widely known, but these two arts do work very well together. Many of the punches, blocks and kicks of karate are contained in *Kodokan* judo, and a number of judo throws are utilized in *Shotokan* karate at an advanced level. There is also a spiritual link between the two arts, in that Dr Kano, the creator of judo, was very friendly with the founder of *Shotokan* karate, Gichin Funakoshi. This relationship involved a mutual exchange of *budo* scientific technique and methods of combat, resulting in some of these being formalized by the *Kodokan*. An expert in traditional judo and *Shotokan* karate would make a formidable opponent in self defence.

Another useful judo-related system of *budo* training is *aikido* (the Way of harmony). Many traditional masters of judo also held similar status in *aikido*, and it is not uncommon for dedicated *budo* enthusiasts to devote their lives to the three arts of judo, *karate* and *aikido*.

Kodokan goshinjutsu

After much research and development by Kano and his colleagues at the *Kodokan*, this system of self defence for *judoka* was finally formalized in 1956. The method includes suitable self defence techniques that can be utilized against grappling, choking, striking or kicking attacks, and there is also a category dealing with defence against the knife, stick and gun.

The art of *goshinjutsu* is a fascinating subject, and advanced *judoka* can spend years perfecting it. Once perfected, it is an excellent form of protection for a practising *judoka*. Techniques of throwing, armlocking, strangling and striking are utilized to great effect.

URBAN STREET FIGHTING AND JUDO

If an attack is unavoidable, physical fitness or some knowledge of self defence, ideally a martial art, will increase the victim's chance of survival. Martial arts training, especially judo, is ideal for this purpose; by its very nature, judo is close-quarter combat, and the effect of judo in self defence can be very dramatic. However, one very important point to remember is that a short course does not create an expert — any form of combat training must be practised regularly, and the repertoire of the practitioner extended.

A sex attacker was left screaming in pain after being thrown by a 13-year-old girl judo exponent. As he pounced on the 155 cm (5 feet 2 inches) youngster in an alley on her way to school, she defended herself by the use of judo. She caught her attacker in a reverse Japanese stranglehold, followed it with an armlock and a throw which sent him flying over her head. As the man, suffering agony from a dislocated shoulder, tried to get to his feet, she grabbed him by the ankle, toppling him a second time before he managed to stagger away, allowing her to run home to alert her mother. This girl had been studying judo for only two years.

A detective in charge of the hunt for the man said 'She is a very brave little girl. She couldn't call for help because a few days earlier she had an accident which had temporarily affected her voice. She did an excellent job of protecting herself against this man, who we are treating as a potential rapist.'

Now, it would be very easy to study the experiences of this 13-year-old and assume that judo is the be all and end all of self defence. This is not the case. There is no such thing as a complete self defence system; the attitude of the victim and the circumstances at the time play a primary role in the final outcome. There are numerous cases of highly qualified martial arts practitioners being caught unawares and injured, or even murdered, by their attackers. The following example describes what happened to a 180 cm (6 feet) female judo black belt police officer who was attacked unexpectedly:

The woman police officer was walking her Rotweiller dog in a park. This highly-experienced judo champion was suddenly confronted by an attacker, who threw her to the ground in a brutal attempt to rape her. She was unable to defend herself against this attack, and if it had not been for her dog (hearing the commotion from some distance away) coming to her assistance there is no telling what would have happened.

When interviewed later, this police officer said 'I just froze, I didn't know what was happening, it didn't occur to me to use any of my judo.'

Many martial artists, including *judoka*, have underestimated the urban street fighter. Once again, an example serves to illuminate the dangers of such negligence:

Two extremely fit and capable martial arts instructors, graded black belt in judo and karate, allowed themselves to become involved in an argument with a gang of troublesome hooligans. A fight developed and, instead of avoiding the confrontation, they engaged in the melée.

Their over-confidence, probably created by too much alcohol, resulted in a good thrashing from the hooligans, followed by several days' hospitalization. Had the martial artists obeyed the golden rule of *zanshin* (awareness), this situation would never have developed. Fortunately, they were not seriously injured.

It should be remembered that, in its own way, street fighting is a scientific art without rules. Practitioners of the urban way can be very vicious, and frequently resort to the use of makeshift weapons as well as knives or possibly guns. Even the *judoka* with years of experience should beware of the streetfighter, who has a very special code — kill or be killed.

To sum up, physically fit *judoka*, from sports or traditional schools, should be capable of defending themselves in an urban environment. However, circumstances and personal attitude will always affect how you defend yourself, so it is impossible for an instructor to give any form of guarantee with judo tuition. The following couple of examples illustrate this point:

A criminal investigator was attempting to serve court

papers on a defendant. This investigator was extremely
fit and highly experienced in judo, karate and *ju-jitsu.*
Generally speaking, he was a man of the world, with
previous service in specialist units of the armed forces. It
would therefore be reasonable to assume his chances of
survival if he was forced to defend himself would be
very good.

Having located the defendant named in the court
papers, the investigator then completed the preamble of
explaining the nature of the charges, whereupon the
defendant became very agitated and threatened
violence.

With service of the papers concluded, the investigator
turned his back on the defendant and began to leave
the premises. The defendant, still screaming threats,
grabbed a claw-hammer and chased after the
investigator, who was by now in the street, walking
away from the scene.

The attacker grabbed the investigator by the arm,
swinging him round. Raising the claw-hammer above
his head, the attacker then hit his victim in the front of
the face, knocking him back against a wall, and
proceeded to deliver a series of blows to the head.
Barely conscious, the victim succeeded in wrapping his
arm around the neck of the assailant, and just managed
to execute a judo hip throw, which resulted in the
attacker falling violently to the ground. If it had not
been for this automatic reaction, who knows what might
have happened to the investigator.

The moral of this story is obvious; such a highly trained
martial arts technician should never have turned his back
on a potential assailant, especially one screaming threats
of violence. This second mistake was in not reacting at the
moment he was swung round by the attacker; at that time
the attacker's arm was raised and about to strike, leaving
enough time to effect a suitable technique.

A young 15-year-old schoolgirl, returning home one

autumn evening, was suddenly confronted by a male assailant who attempted to drag her into a tree-lined garden. Her immediate reaction was to punch him extremely hard on the nose, which caused him to release his grip. She then placed both her hands on his shoulders and pushed him over a garden wall, into some flowerbeds, where he lay, quite dazed. The young girl then ran to a nearby house, where she called for help. The residents were able to apprehend the attacker and deliver him to the police.

This young girl had never received any form of self defence training in her life, yet she was able to respond in this positive way. When interviewed, she simply described her fears of being attacked and how she was aware of the possibility of such a thing happening to her.

Ironically, the assailant, when charged, admitted to a series of previous violent attacks on over 11 women, some of whom had attended self-defence courses.

These two final examples should serve to remind all martial arts practitioners that, no matter how experienced they may be, commonsense and awareness must be applied to everyday life.

8
JUDO, CHILDREN AND THE DISABLED

CHILDREN AND JUDO

Hundreds of thousands of children all over the world regularly enjoy the rough and tumble of judo. Their natural sense of adventure, with the urge to engage in combat-style games, enables them to devote maximum effort to the physical aspects of training.

It is highly unlikely that these young practitioners fully understand the history or philosophy of their chosen Way. However, in countries where judo is compulsory within the education system, lectures are given on these important areas and it is pleasantly surprising to find youngsters with an enthusiasm for the background to their art.

Lack of philosophical or historical knowledge does not really create a problem for the junior adept. As long as lessons are conducted in the traditional manner, with a strict code of behaviour and discipline, then academic aspects of judo can be injected into lessons over a period of time.

Tournaments and children

A certain amount of competition is healthy for a child. However, parents and instructors who encourage young *judoka* in the stresses of regular competition are not, in the opinion of some experts, contributing to overall development.

Some judo organizations regularly organize tournaments for very small children weighing under 25 kg! Sometimes these youngsters are only seven or eight years old, and very inexperienced. It should be appreciated that the bodies of these children are still developing; to expose them to the regular effects of sporting tournaments before this cycle is complete is most unwise.

Furthermore, in a number of Western competitions judo coaches, as well as parents, have been observed shouting unorthodox advice to their fledglings, in a desperate attempt to encourage contest success. This is intolerable behaviour which has no place in a traditional environment.

Benefits for children

Carefully controlled, however, judo can be of tremendous benefit to children. By adopting the traditional *Kodokan* principles, youngsters from the age of seven years can enjoy an activity that will enable them to exhaust their natural urges as well as all their physical energy, and at the same time mould them into disciplined respectable junior members of society.

At such an early age, children are unable to identify the benefits gained from their judo — they simply enjoy their lessons and display continuing enthusiasm for what they believe is merely a sport. The communal activity of the sport is an excellent method of overall development for a child, with increased alertness created by *randori*, as well as the occasional competition stimulating mental activity. This is bound to have a beneficial effect on the practitioner.

Parents invariably report pleasant changes of personality and conduct in their children. There is also evidence of increased confidence, as well as academic improvements in other subjects. This particularly applies to Western children, whose educational system is different to that of Japan. For example, the parents of two young children wrote a letter of gratitude to a Western martial arts coach and his wife, who had been responsible for the judo education of their children. The contents of this letter aptly describe the benefits that a child can receive from training in the gentle Way.

> Just a short line to say 'thank you' and express our appreciation for you giving up a whole week of your valuable time so that Helen and David could learn more about judo. They also had a lot of fun, as well as increasing in self confidence.
>
> There is such a great need today in our materialistic world, where everyone is selfishly rushing around pleasing themselves, both for people to give themselves (their time, energy and care), and for children to see this happening. Helen and David have learnt much more than just judo this week and we hope that, through seeing you both give your time to help them they will, in their turn, be more willing to give themselves when the opportunity presents itself. Once again, our warm thanks to you both.
>
> God bless you.

Techniques for children

Whilst many of the teachings of judo can be adopted by junior practitioners, it is important to appreciate that certain throws, armlocks and strangulations should not be introduced until the child has reached maturity/young adulthood. The reasons for this should be obvious. Parents are therefore advised to investigate methods of tuition in use before submitting their children to a particular club. As with adults, *ukemi* (breakfalling) should be an integral part of initial basic training.

Newaza (grappling) is a useful exercise for children and can be utilized, along with a number of interesting 'judo games'. Mr Toni Goffe of the British Judo Association is to be congratulated for his contribution in this direction.

Ippon Seoi-nage (one-arm shoulder throw) — suitable for all ages.

O-goshi (major hip throw) — suitable for all ages.

JUDO IN JAPANESE SCHOOLS

In Japan all children receive tuition in at least one martial art during their early days of education, judo being perhaps the most popular. This usually continues out of junior school and into high school and university, by which time practitioners have attained an advanced ability. This system of education is invaluable to youngsters, who may or may not continue with their *budo* studies upon graduation. Whatever decision they make, their basic grounding in discipline and etiquette will contribute to their future.

Examples of Japan's young *judoka* who have benefited from junior martial arts tuition can be seen in Yosuke Yamamoto, 5th *dan*, and Toshihiko Koga, 3rd *dan*, who are the two top competitors leading the new generation of Japan's judo fighters. Yamamoto, a teacher, and Koga, a 21-year-old junior, both of Nihon College of Physical Education, are two of a kind, who out-manoeuvre large opponents with their laser-sharp skills, developed during their junior years.

JUDO FOR THE PHYSICALLY DISABLED

A number of judo instructors and organizations have undertaken to teach the art to physically disabled persons. Whilst one's immediate reaction to this idea might be less than enthusiastic, the evidence of successes points to a more positive attitude being needed towards such a scheme.

The blind

Over the years partially-sighted as well as totally blind people have been attracted to judo. Their inability to see enhances their sensitivity in other directions, which is invaluable to the execution of actual techniques. There are many blind practitioners engaged in judo practice; for example, at the Para-Olympics of 1988 16-year-old brown belt Simon Jackson of Great Britain won a gold medal by beating his black belt opponent.

The courage of blind *judoka* is to be admired. There are very few special facilities for these people, who simply find themselves having to fit into the general run of things. Despite these inconveniences, a majority of the blind enjoy their training and benefit in a number of ways.

Other disabilities

The expression 'judo is for everyone' includes individuals who may be unfortunate enough to suffer from more complicated physical disabilities, such as missing limbs, partial paralysis, or medical conditions resulting in general malfunctioning of the body.

There are a number of such people regularly practising martial arts including judo and, whilst they obviously will never become champions or perhaps black belts, they benefit in many ways that cannot be described by someone outside their environment. As far as dedicated traditional coaches are concerned, such people are more than welcome to attend lessons, where every effort will be made to assist them.

9
EPILOGUE

In 1932, at the University of Southern California, Los
Angeles, the founder of judo, Dr Jigoro Kano, delivered a
lengthy address entitled 'The Contribution of Judo to
Education'. This paper is an illuminating insight to the
mind of a man whose roots lay in the world of the
Japanese *samurai* warrior. It describes how Dr Kano
transformed the lethal art of *ju-jitsu* into judo (the gentle
Way), a physical educational activity that could be
enjoyed by anyone. 'The Contribution of Judo to
Education' is, in effect, a kind of martial artists' bible
that should be retained and regularly studied by all
judoka of every rank.

'THE CONTRIBUTION OF JUDO TO EDUCATION' BY JIGORO KANO

The object of this lecture is to explain to you, in a general
way what judo is. In our feudal times there were many
military exercises such as fencing, archery, the use of
spears, etc. Among them was one called *ju-jitsu*, a
composite exercise consisting principally of the way of
fighting without weapons, though daggers, swords and
other weapons were occasionally used.

The kinds of attack were chiefly throwing, hitting,
choking, holding the opponent down, and bending or
twisting the opponent's arms or legs in such a way as to
cause pain or fracture. The use of swords and daggers was
also taught. We also had multitudinous ways of defending
ourselves against such attacks. Such exercise, in its
primitive form, existed even in our mythological age. But
systematic instruction in it, as an art, dates only from
about 350 years ago.

Giving way

In my young days I studied this art with three eminent masters of the time. The great benefit I derived from the study of it led me to make up my mind to go on with the subject more seriously, and in 1882 I started a school of my own and called it *Kodokan*. Literally, *Kodokan* means 'a school for studying the Way', 'the Way' being the concept of life itself. I named the subject that I teach 'judo' instead of *ju-jitsu*. First, I shall give you the meaning of these words. *Ju* means 'gentle' or 'to give way', *jitsu* means 'art' or 'principle'. Thus *ju-jitsu* means an art or practice in gentleness, or means first giving way in order ultimately to gain the victory; 'judo' on the other hand, means the way or principle of that same procedure.

Let me now explain what this gentleness or giving way really means. Let's assume that we can estimate a man's strength in units. Let's say that the strength of a man standing in front of me is represented by 10 units, where my strength — less than his — is represented by 7 units. Then if he pushes me with all his force, I shall certainly be pushed or thrown down, even if I use all my strength against him, opposing strength with strength. But if, instead, I were to give way to his strength by withdrawing my body just as he pushed, remembering at the same time to keep my balance, then he would naturally lean forward and thus lose his balance.

In this new position he may have become so weak (not in actual physical strength, but because of his awkward position) as to have his strength represented, for the moment, by 3 units instead of his normal 10. Meanwhile, by keeping my balance, I retain my full strength — this is, half my 7 units, or 3½ against his 3. That would leave half of my strength available for any purpose. In case I had greater strength than my opponent, I would of course push him back. But even in this case — this is, if I wished to push him back and had the power to do so — it would be better first for me to give way because by so doing I could greatly economize my energy.

This is one simple instance of how an opponent can be

beaten if one gives way. Other examples can be given.
Suppose that an opponent tries to twist my body
intending to cause me to fall down. If I were to resist him,
I should surely be thrown down, because my strength is not
sufficient to overcome his. But if, on the other hand, I gave
way to him, and while doing so pulled him, throwing my body
voluntarily to the ground, I could throw him very easily.

I'll give another example. Suppose that we were walking
along a mountain road with a precipice on one side, and
that a man suddenly sprang upon me and tried to push
me down the precipice. In this case I couldn't help being
pushed over the precipice if I attempted to resist him, but
on the contrary, if I gave way to him and at the same time
turned my body around and pulled my opponent towards
the precipice, I could easily throw him over the edge and
at the same time throw my own body safely to the ground.

I could multiply these examples endlessly, but I think
the ones I have given will help you understand how I can
beat an opponent by giving way. There are many
instances where this principle is applied in *ju-jitsu*
contests, and the name *ju-jitsu*, meaning the gentle or the
giving way art, came to be the name of the whole art.

Maximum efficiency

But strictly speaking, real *ju-jitsu* is something more. *Ju-
jitsu* is not confined to gaining victory only by giving way.
We sometimes hit, kick and choke in physical contests,
and in contradistinction to giving way, such actions are
forms of direct attack.

Sometimes an opponent takes hold of one's wrist. How
can one possibly release oneself without using his strength
against his opponent's grip? The same thing can be asked
when somebody grips him from behind. If the principle of
giving way cannot cover all of the methods used in a
ju-jitsu contest, is there any principle that really covers
the whole field? Yes, there is, and it is the principle of
maximum efficient use of mind and body. *Ju-jitsu* is
nothing but an application of this all-pervading principle
in attack and defence.

Can this principle be applied to other fields of human activity? Yes, this same principle can be applied to the improvement of the human body, making it strong, healthy and useful. Thus it is the basic principle of physical education. It can also be applied to the improvement of intellectual and moral power, and in this way it constitutes mental and moral education. At the same time it can be applied to the improvement of diet, clothing, housing, social intercourse and methods of business, thus constituting training in living. I gave the name of 'judo' to this all-pervading principle. So 'judo' in its fuller sense, is a means of training both mind and body in the regulation of life and affairs.

In one of its phases, judo can be studied and practised with attack and defence as its main object. Before I started the *Kodokan,* that attack and defence phase of judo was studied and practised in Japan under the name *ju-jitsu* (or sometimes *tai-jitsu,* meaning the art of managing the body, or *yawara,* the gentle management). But I came to think that the study of this all-pervading principle is more important than the practice of mere *ju-jitsu,* because really understanding the principle not only enables one to apply it to all phases of life, but also it is of great service in the study of the art of *ju-jitsu* itself.

It's not only through the process I took that one can come to grasp this principle. One can arrive at the same conclusion by philosophical interpretation of the daily transaction of business, or through abstract philosophical reasoning. But when I started to teach judo, I thought it advisable to follow the same course that I had taken in the study of the subject because by so doing I could make the body of my pupil healthy, strong and useful. At the same time, I could assist him gradually in grasping this all-important principle. For that reason, I began judo instruction with training in *randori* and *kata.*

Judo in physical education

Randori — meaning free exercise — is practised under actual contest conditions. It includes throwing, choking, holding an opponent down, and bending or twisting his arms and legs. The two combatants may use whatever methods they like, provided they don't hurt each other and provided they obey the rules of judo etiquette, which are essential to its proper working.

Kata — literally meaning 'form' — is a system of pre-arranged exercises, including hitting, kicking, cutting, thrusting, etc., according to rules under which each combatant knows beforehand exactly what his opponent is going to do. The training in hitting, kicking, cutting and thrusting are given in *kata* and not in *randori* because if they were used in *randori* there might frequently be injuries. In *kata*, injuries are unlikely because all the attacks and defences are pre-arranged.

Randori may be practised in various ways. If the object is simply training in methods of attack and defence, attention should be directed especially to the most efficient ways of throwing, bending, or twisting, without special reference to developing the body or to mental and moral culture.

Randori can also be undertaken with physical education as its main object. From what I have already said, it should be obvious that maximum efficiency should be the objective whenever one performs anything. We shall see how the existing systems of physical education can stand this test. Talking of athletics as a whole, I cannot help thinking that they are not the ideal form of physical education because every movement isn't chosen for the all-round development of the body, but rather for attaining some other definite objective.

Furthermore, since we gradually require special equipment for athletics and sometimes quite a number of persons participate in them, athletics are suited to the training of selected groups of persons but not as a means of improving the physical condition of a whole nation. This holds true of boxing, wrestling and different kinds of military exercises practised all over the world.

The people may ask, 'Aren't gymnastics an ideal form of national physical training?' To this, I answer that they are an ideal form of physical education in that they are contrived for all-round development of the body and don't necessarily require special equipment and many participants, but gymnastics lack very important things essential to the physical education of a whole nation. The defects are:

- Different gymnastic movements have no meaning and naturally are devoid of interest.
- No secondary benefit can be derived from them.
- Unlike some other exercises, gymnastics don't confer 'skill' (in the special meaning of 'skill').

From this brief survey of the whole field of physical education, I can say that no ideal form has yet been invented to meet the necessary conditions for such physical education. That ideal form can be devised only from a study based on maximum efficiency. To fulfil all those conditions and requirements, a system of all-round development of the body must be devised, as in the case of gymnastics. Next, the movements should have some meaning, so that they can be engaged in with interest. Again, the activities should require no large space, special dress or equipment. Furthermore, they must be such as can be done by individuals as well as by groups.

Those are the conditions or requirements for a satisfactory system of physical education for a whole nation. Any system that can meet those requirements successfully for a whole nation may, for the first time, be regarded as a programme of physical education based on the principle of maximum efficiency.

I have been studying this subject for a long time and have succeeded in devising two forms which may be said to fulfil all those requirements. One of them is what I have named the 'representative form'. It is a way of representing ideas, emotions and different motions of natural objects by the movements of the limbs, body and neck. Dancing is one such activity, but originally dancing wasn't devised with physical education as its objective, and therefore cannot be said to fulfil all of the requirements. But it is possible to devise special kinds of dancing to suit persons of differing sexes and mental and physical conditions and to express moral ideas and feelings. Thus, conjointly with the cultivation of the spiritual side of a nation, dancing can be made to develop the body in a way suited to all.

This 'representative form', I believe, is practised in one way or another in America and Europe, and you can, I think, imagine what I mean. Therefore, I'll not deal with it any further here.

There is one other form that I named the 'attack and defence form'. In it, I have combined different methods of attack and defence in such a way as to conduce the harmonious development of the whole body. Ordinary methods of attack and defence taught in *ju-jitsu* can't be considered ideal for the development of the body. Therefore, I have combined them especially to fulfil the conditions necessary for the harmonious development of the body. This combination can be said to satisfy two purposes: (1) bodily development; and (2) training in the art of contest. Just as every nation must provide for national defence, so every individual must know how to defend himself. In this age of enlightenment, nobody would care to prepare either for national aggression or for doing individual violence to others. But defence, in the cause of justice and humanity, must never be neglected by a nation or by an individual.

This 'attack and defence form' of physical education, I shall show you in actual practice. It is divided into two kinds of exercise with an opponent. [There then followed a demonstration of what Dr Kano meant.]

From what I have explained and shown you in practice, you no doubt understand what I mean by physical education based on the principle of maximum efficiency. Although I strongly believe that the physical education of a whole nation should be conducted on that principle, I don't mean to under-emphasise athletics and the various kinds of martial exercise. Although they cannot be deemed appropriate as physical education for a whole nation, yet they have their special value as a culture for a group or persons, and I have no wish to discourage them, especially in *randori* and judo.

One great value of *randori* lies in the abundance of movements it affords of physical development. Another value is that every movement has some purpose and is executed with spirit, whereas ordinary gymnastic exercises lack interest. The object of systematic physical training in judo is not only to develop the body but to enable a man or a woman to have perfect control over mind and body, and to make him or her ready to meet any emergency, whether it is a pure accident or an attack by others.

Another exercise in judo is generally conducted by two persons in *kata* and in *randori*, and usually in a room specially prepared for the purpose. It can be practised by a group or by a single person, on a playground or in an ordinary room. People imagine that falling, in *randori*, is attended by pain and sometimes by danger. But a brief explanation of the way one is taught to fall will make clear that there is no such pain or danger.

I shall now speak of the intellectual phase of judo. Mental training in judo can be achieved by *kata* as well as by *randori*, but more successfully by the latter. Since *randori* is competition between two persons, using all the resources at their command and obeying the prescribed rules of judo, both people must always be wide awake, looking for the weak points of the opponent, and ready to attack whenever opportunity allows. Such an attitude of mind in devising means of attack makes the pupil earnest, sincere, thoughtful, cautious and deliberate in all his dealings. At the same time, he is trained for quick decision and prompt action because unless one decides quickly and acts promptly in *randori*, he always loses his opportunity either in attacking or in defence.

Again, in *randori* a contestant can't tell what his opponent is going to do, so he must always be prepared to meet any sudden attack. Habituated to that kind of mental attitude, he develops a high degree of mental composure — of poise. Exercise of power of attention and observation in the gymnasium naturally develops that power and it is very useful in daily life.

Exercise of the power of imagination, of reasoning and of judgment is indispensable in devising a means of defeating an opponent, and such a power is naturally developed in *randori*. Again, since *randori* involves the relations — mental and physical — existing between two competitors, hundreds of valuable lessons can be derived from such exercise, but I'll content myself for the present by giving a few examples. In *randori* we teach the pupil always to act on the fundamental principle of judo, no matter how physically inferior his opponent may seem, because an opponent will never be convinced of his defeat, no matter what brutal strength may have been used on him. It is hardly necessary to point out that the way to convince an opponent in an argument is not to push this or that advantage over him, be it derived from power, from knowledge or from wealth, but to persuade him in accordance with the inviolable rules of logic. The lesson that persuasion, not coercion, is efficacious — which is so valuable in actual life — we can learn from *randori*.

Again, we teach the learner that when he has recourse to any trick in overcoming an opponent, he should employ only as much force as is absolutely required for his purpose, and caution him against either an over- or under-exertion of force. There are many cases in which people fail in what they undertake simply because they go too far, not knowing where to stop, or *vice-versa*.

To take still another instance, we teach the learner in *randori* that when he faces an opponent who is madly excited he must score a victory over him, not by resisting him directly with might and main, but by playing him till his fury exhausts him and he expends himself.

The usefulness of this attitude in everyday transactions with others is patent. As is well known, no amount of reasoning can avail us when we are confronted by a person who is so agitated as to seem to have lost his temper. All we have to do in such a case is to wait until his passion wears itself out. All these teachings we can learn from the practice of *randori*. Their application to the conduct of daily affairs is a very interesting study, and is valuable as an intellectual training for young minds.

I'll finish my talk about the intellectual phase of judo by referring briefly to the national means of increasing knowledge and intellectual power. If we observe society closely, we notice everywhere the way in which we expend our energy foolishly in the acquisition of knowledge. Our surroundings are always giving us opportunities to gain useful knowledge, but aren't we constantly neglecting the best use of such opportunities? Are we always making the best choice of books, magazines and newspapers? Don't we often find out that the energy which might have been spent in acquiring useful knowledge is really used in amassing knowledge which is prejudicial not only to ourselves but also to society.

Besides acquiring useful knowledge, we must endeavour to improve our intellectual powers such as memory, attention, observation, judgment, reasoning, imagination, etc. This we should not do in a haphazard manner, but in accordance with psychological laws, so that the relation of those powers, one with another, will be well harmonized. It is only by faithfully following the principle of maximum efficiency — in other words, the principle of judo — that we can achieve the objective, of rationally increasing our knowledge and intellectual power.

Moral discipline

I shall now speak about the moral phase of judo. It isn't my intention to speak of the moral discipline given to students in the exercise room, such as the observance of the regular rules of etiquette, courage and perseverance, kindness and respect for others, impartiality and fair play so much emphasized in athletic sports throughout the world. Training in judo has a special moral import in Japan because judo, together with other martial exercises,

was practised by our *samurai* who had a high code of
honour, the spirit of which has been bequeathed to us
through the teaching of the art.

In this connection, I wish to explain how the principle of
maximum efficiency helps us in promoting moral conduct.
A man is sometimes very excitable and prone to anger for
trivial reasons, but when one comes to consider that
excitement is an unnecessary expenditure of energy,
giving benefit to nobody but often doing harm, it will be
seen that students of judo refrain from such conduct.

From disappointment, a man is sometimes despondent,
is gloomy and has no courage to work. To such a man,
judo comes with the advice that he should find out what is
the best thing to do under the existing circumstances.
Paradoxical as it may seem, such a man is, to my mind in
the same position as one who is at the zenith of success. In
either case, there is only one course to follow — what, after
due consideration he deems to be the best course of action
at the time. Thus the teaching of judo can be said to lead
a man from the depths of disappointment and lethargy to
a state of vigorous activity, with a bright hope for the
future.

The same reasoning applies to persons who are
discontented. They are often in a sulky state of mind, and
blame other people for what is their own fault, without
attending to their own business. Judo will make such
persons understand that such conduct is contrary to the
principle of maximum efficiency, and will make them
realize that by faithful pursuit of that principle they can
become more cheerful. Thus judo is serviceable in a
variety of ways to the promotion of moral conduct.

Emotional aspect
Finally, I wish to add a few words about the emotional
phase of judo. We all are aware of the pleasurable
sensation that exercise gives to the nerves and muscles,
and we also feel pleasure at the attainment of skill in the
use of our muscles and in overcoming others in contests.
But besides these pleasures there is a love of beauty and

delight derivable from assuming graceful attitudes and performing graceful movements, as well as seeing the same things done by other people. The training in these, together with the pleasure obtainable from watching movements symbolizing various ideas, constitutes what we call the emotional or aesthetic phase of judo.

I believe you have come to see, by this time, what kind of thing judo really is, in contradistinction to the *ju-jitsu* of feudal times. It can be summed up as follows. Judo is a study and a training in mind and body, as well as in the regulation of one's life and affairs. From the thorough study of the various methods of attack and defence, I became convinced that they all depend on the application of one all-pervading principle, namely 'Whatever be the object, it can best be attained by the highest or maximum-efficient use of mind and body for that purpose.' Just as that principle applied to methods of attack and defence constitutes *ju-jitsu*, so does the same principle applied to physical, mental and moral culture, as well as ways of living and business affairs, constitute the study of and training in those things. Once the real import of this principle is understood, it can be applied to all phases of life and activity, and it enables one to lead the highest and most rational life.

The real understanding of this principle need not necessarily be arrived at through training in the methods of attack and defence, but as I came to conceive of this idea through training in these methods, I made such training in competition and training for the development of the body the regular means of arriving at the principle.

This principle of maximum-efficiency, when applied to the keying-up or perfecting of social life, just as when applied to the coordination of mind and body in the science of attack and defence, demands, first of all, order and harmony among its members, and this can be attained only through mutual aid and concession, leading to mutual welfare and benefit.

The final aim of judo, therefore, is to inculcate in the mind of man a spirit of respect for the principle of maximum efficiency and of mutual welfare and benefit, leading him so to practise them that man — individually and collectively — can attain the highest skill in attack and defence.

If we closely observe the actual state of society all over the world — notwithstanding the fact that morality in all its forms (religious, philosophical and traditional) is meant to improve man's conduct in society and to make the world ideal — we see that present circumstances are quite the contrary. We see vices, quarrels and discontent in every level of society, from the highest to the lowest. Although we are taught hygiene and correct ways of living in school, from childhood to maturity, we still are prone to neglect the rules of clean living and of hygienic, orderly lives.

The actual facts prove that our society is lacking in something which, if brought to light and universal knowledge, can remodel the present society and bring greater happiness and satisfaction to the world. This is the teaching of maximum efficiency and mutual welfare and benefit.

I don't mean to say that our time-honoured moral precepts and hygienics should be shelved. On the contrary, let those precepts and advice be ever respected, as they used to be, but in addition to these, our principle of maximum efficiency and mutual welfare and benefit should be ever paramount. This I say emphatically, because if any teaching is to have effect in this age of criticism and new ideas, it must have some indubitable reason or fact behind it.

The thinking man today doesn't say 'Because I believe in such and such a thing, therefore you must believe in it' or 'I came to such and such a conclusion through my own reasoning, and no sane person can deny or doubt it.' Certainly, however, none can deny the value of the principle 'Whatever be the object, it can best be attained through the highest on maximally-efficient use of mind and body for that purpose'.

Again, none can deny that it is only by aiming at

mutual welfare and benefit that every member of society can keep from discord and quarrelling, and live in peace and prosperity. Is it not because of the universal recognition of those facts that people have come to talk so much about efficiency and scientific management and that everywhere they are being advocated?

In addition to this, the principle of give-and-take is more and more coming to be the determining factor in the lives of all human beings. Is it not because of this principle of mutual welfare and benefit that we came to form the League of Nations and that the great powers of the world met for the decrease of naval and military armaments?

Those movements are also automatic acknowledgments of the crying need for efficiency and mutual welfare and benefit. They must be fostered by the educational forces of every country, and judo should have a principal role in achieving them.

POSTSCRIPT – BACK TO SQUARE ONE

It was recently announced in Japan that the training methods used by the Japanese national team are to be changed. It would appear that since experiencing a disastrous defeat in the Seoul Olympics in 1988, in which only one gold medal was won, the team authorities have decided to return to square one, and to seek the fundamental principles of the art and its founder, Jigoro Kano. And a most refreshing article in the April 1989 issue of Japan's prestigious international *Judo* magazine is a comprehensive story of Jigoro Kano, referred to as 'the Superman', the founding father of judo.

GLOSSARY

To retain the traditional methods and values of judo is
very important. To allow distortion or eventual decline of
this fascinating martial art would be a grave injustice.
Jigoro Kano and his loyal confederates travelled the world
in an attempt to disseminate a way of life that is designed
to create peace and cooperation amongst mankind. This
was indeed a difficult task, primarily because of the
language and cultural difficulties experienced in the
various countries.

One method adopted by Dr Kano was to utilize
Japanese terminology when describing the various judo
techniques. These names are still used today, despite a
number of attempts to abort this system of teaching. It is
therefore important for all *judoka* to remember and use
the following Japanese terminology throughout their judo
lifetime. (Japanese terminology used in competitions is
excluded from this list.)

aikido Way of Harmony.
atemi-waza Striking techniques.
budo Martial Way.
budoka Practitioner of martial arts.
bushido Way of the warrior.
dan Black belt grade.
do Way, or path.
dojo Place of practising the Way.
goshinjutsu Kodokan method of self defence.
hajime Referee terminology — begin.
hara Stomach, centre of energy.
ippon Maximum points win.
judo Gentle Way.
judogi Judo costume.
judoka Person practising judo.

ju-jitsu *Samurai* method of unarmed combat, before judo.

kansetsu-waza Armlocking techniques.

karate Empty hand.

kata Pre-arranged form.

katsu Method of resuscitation.

kendo Way of the Sword.

ki Spiritual energy.

kiai A cry designed to create energy and instil fear in an opponent.

Kodokan Place for studying the way.

kuzushi Breaking of opponent's balance.

kyu-do Archery way.

makiwara Striking board.

mokusu Meditation.

muju Impermanence or death.

newaza Grappling on the ground.

obi Belt.

osaekomi-waza Holding techniques.

randori Free practice.

rei Salutation, bow.

samurai Japanese knight or warrior.

sensei Teacher or instructor.

shime-waza Strangulation techniques.

sho-shin Beginner's mind.

tachi-waza Standing techniques (throws).

tai-sabaki Body movements.

tatami Judo mats.

ukemi Art of breakfalling.

zanshin Awareness, the watchful, unattached mind.

zazen Meditation.

REFERENCE SECTION

BIBLIOGRAPHY

Alan Fromm and Nicholas Soames, *Judo — The Gentle Way*, Routledge & Kegan Paul, London, 1982.

Tony Reay and Geoffrey Hobbs, *The Judo Manual*, Barrie & Jenkins, London, 1979.

Taisen Deshimaru, *The Zen Way to Martial Arts*, Rider, London, 1983.

G. Koizumi, *My Study of Judo*, Foulsham, Slough, 1960.

Shinzo Takagaki, *The Techniques of Judo*, Tuttle, Tokyo and Vermont, 1957.

Risei Kano, *Illustrated Kodokan Judo*, Kodansha, Tokyo, 1955.

Minoru Mochizuki, *Fighting Arts International*, Terry O'Neill, Liverpool, 1988.

PROFESSIONAL ORGANIZATIONS

All *bona fide* clubs are members of their country's federation or association responsible for the control and development of judo. Traditional, as well as sporting, establishments are included in these organizations and it is up to the potential practitioner to select a club appropriate to personal requirements.

Whatever style is chosen, the traditional roots of this fascinating martial art must never be forgotten. Without this consideration, the efforts of Dr Kano and the *Kodokan* will be forgotten, and this would be completely contrary to the spirit of the gentle Way.

Britain
British Judo Association
9 Islington High Street
London N1 9LQ
01-833 4424

Belgium
Ligue Belge de Judo et DA
rue General Thijs 15
B-1050 Bruxelles
(2) 648-76-52

France
Federation Française de Judo et DA
43 rue des Plantes
F-75680 Paris Cedex 14
(1) 4-542-80-90

Holland
Judo Bond Nederland
Blokhoeve 5
Postbus 7012
NL-3430 NL Nieuwegein
(3402) 38-114

Italy
Federazione Italiana Judo
Viale Tiziano 70
I-00100 Roma
(6) 368-58-2931

West Germany
Deutscher Judo-Bund ev
Lessingstrasse 12
Postfach 1749
D-6500 Mainz 1
(6131) 67-20-31

Australia
Judo Federation of Australia
12 Forestway
French's Forest
Sydney 2086
New South Wales
(02) 451-6311

Canada
Judo Canada (CKBBA)
333 River Road
Vanier
Ontario K1L 8H9

Egypt
Egyptian Judo Federation
17 El Samman St
8th Zone
Egypt
261-3298 and 391-6613

New Zealand
New Zealand Judo Federation
145 Calliope Road
Stanley Bay
Auckland 9
450-341

USA
United States Judo Inc.
PO Box 637
El Paso
Texas 79944
(915) 541-7393

China
People's Republic of China Chinese Judo Association
c/o Chinese Olympic Committee
9 Tiyuguan Road
Beijing

Japan
All Japan Judo Federation
c/o *Kodokan* Judo Institute
16–30 Kasuga 1-chome
Bunkyo-ku
Tokyo
(03) 811-7151

Hong Kong
Hong Kong Judo Association
PO Box 2888
GPO Hong Kong
(3) 681335

Singapore
Singapore Judo Federation
Portsdown Road
Singapore 0513
4756406

Africa
African Judo Union
2 rue Caporal Grebert
Casablanca
Morocco

INDEX

Page numbers in *italic* refer to illustrations.